ANCIENT AFRICAN CIVILIZATIONS

Columns at Musawwarat

ANCIENT AFRICAN CIVILIZATIONS

KUSH AND AXUM

Stanley Burstein
EDITOR

 Markus Wiener Publishers
Princeton

© COPYRIGHT 1998 BY STANLEY BURSTEIN

FOR INFORMATION WRITE TO:
MARKUS WIENER PUBLISHERS
231 NASSAU STREET, PRINCETON, NJ 08542

LIBRARY OF CONGRESS CATALOGING-IN-PUBLICATION DATA

ANCIENT AFRICAN CIVILIZATIONS: KUSH AND AXUM/
STANLEY BURSTEIN, EDITOR
INCLUDES BIBLIOGRAPHICAL REFERENCES AND INDEX.
ISBN 1-55876-147-0 (HC) ISBN 1-55876-148-9 (PB)
1. NUBIA—HISTORY.
2. ASKUM (ETHIOPIA)—HISTORY.
I. BURSTEIN, STANLEY MAYER.
DT159.6.N83A53   1997
939'.78—DC21   97-41207   CIP

BOOK DESIGN BY CHERYL MIRKIN

PRINTED IN THE UNITED STATES OF AMERICA

CONTENTS

ACKNOWLEDGMENTS

This work could not have been completed without the assistance of numerous persons. Acknowledging my debts to them is a pleasant task. Thanks are, of course, first and foremost due to the various publishers and scholars who generously granted me permission to use their translations. I should also like to express my gratitude to Professors Steven Sidebotham of the University of Delaware and David W. Phillipson of Cambridge University and to the British Museum and the Museum of Fine Arts Boston for allowing me to reproduce their excellent photographs of Nubian and Axumite monuments. Dr. Antonio Lopreino, Professor of Egyptology at the University of California at Los Angeles, has repeatedly saved me from embarrassing errors with his sage advice on all matters Egyptian. Finally, the success of this book owes much to the many Nubian scholars who years ago welcomed an interloping Greek historian into their company and have patiently answered his questions ever since.

INTRODUCTION

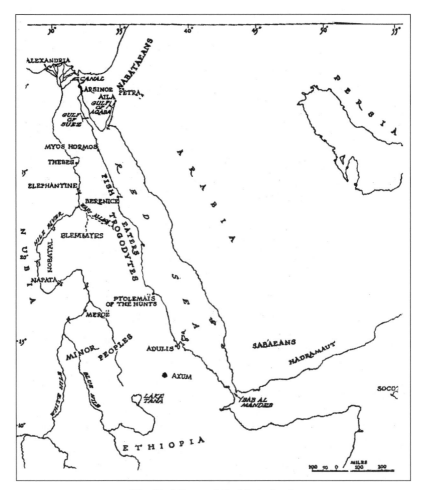

The Red Sea and its hinterlands

KUSH AND AXUM

When most people think of ancient African civilizations, they think of Egypt. The reaction is understandable. Already in antiquity the great age of Egyptian civilization, its fabled wealth, and the grandeur of its monuments awed its neighbors as, indeed, they still awe contemporary visitors to the Nile valley. Not surprisingly, Jews and Greeks tried to connect their own cultures to the immensely more ancient culture of Egypt. Moses and Plato are only two of the founding fathers of Jewish and Greek culture reputed to have visited Egypt. The effort to forge links between Egypt and Western civilization continues even today. For much of the past decade fierce controversy has swirled around the question of Egyptian influence on Greek culture, and it shows no sign of abating.[1] Yet this obsession with Egypt, however understandable it may be, obscures an important point: Egypt was not the only ancient African civilization. For much of antiquity, Egypt shared Northeast Africa with two other great African civilizations: Kush and Axum. The purpose of this book is to provide students and teachers of African history with a documentary history of these two ancient African civilizations at the height of their power and splendor from the third century B.C.E. to the seventh century C.E.

Kush and its Place in History[2]

Kush is the term the ancient Egyptians used to designate the upper Nile Valley south of Egypt and the various civilized states that occupied part or all of that region from the early second millennium B.C.E. to the end of antiquity. The historical significance of these states is considerable. By the early first millennium B.C.E. they had succeeded in unifying virtually the whole of the Nile Valley from near the southern border of contemporary Egypt at Wadi Halfa to a still undetermined point south of Khartoum, the capital of the modern Republic of Sudan. They had also established a tradition of literate civilization supported by irrigation agriculture in the northern portion and a combination of a rain-based agriculture and transhumant pastoralism in the southern portion of that territory that continues to the present day, making the Sudan the oldest continuous center of civilized life in the interior of Africa.

The cultural achievements of the people of Kush were equally impressive. On the basis of the Egyptian hieroglyphic writing system, they created an alphabet which is the only ancient one independent of the Phoenician alphabet that is the ancestor of all those now in use. In addition, the Kushites left a rich artistic legacy that includes one of the most attractive traditions of decorated pottery to appear in the ancient world. They were also responsible for introducing into and firmly establishing in the Upper Nile Valley and its adjacent hinterlands the tradition of iron metallurgy that still exists there today. Finally, Kush and its Medieval successors played a central role in an international trading system that extended from southeast Asia to the Mediterranean.

Kush and its last and most famous capital, the city of Meroë (located near the junction of the Nile and the Atbara rivers in the central Sudan), were well known to the Greeks and Romans under the name Aithiopia ("land of the burnt faced people").[3] Greek writers made it the home of astrology and told of a romance between Alexander the Great and the Queen of Meroë, Jewish writers claimed that Moses' Kushite wife and the Queen of Sheba were both members of the Meroitic royal family, and Christian evangelists counted a Meroitic royal official among the earliest converts to the new faith.

Ancient and Medieval historians, however, knew little of the actual facts of Kushite history. Even the location of Meroë itself was forgotten until the Scottish explorer James Bruce, the discoverer of the Ethiopian source of the Nile, identified its ruins in 1772 on his return to Europe from Ethiopia. Throughout the nineteenth century a series of travelers and adventurers, sometimes at the risk of their lives, visited the territory of Kush and described the remains of its temples and cities. At the same time, the decipherment of Egyptian hieroglyphics illuminated over two millennia of Egyptian involvement in Kush. The writing of a history of Kush itself became possible only in the twentieth century when archaeologists identified and excavated some of the most important centers of Kushite civilization including its three capitals—Kerma, Napata, and Meroë—and their associated cemeteries as well as numerous less important sites.

The Historiography of Kush

The reconstruction of the history of Kush is one of the triumphs of twentieth century historiography, but it is a history of an unfamiliar type. Long-forgotten figures have regained their rightful place in the historical record. Because of the uneven distribution of textual evidence, the best known examples date from the earlier periods of Kushite history. They include the intrepid Egyptian explorer Harkhuf, who boasted in his tomb inscription how he brought a dwarf to the boy king Pepi II about 2236 B.C.E., and the horse-loving Kushite king

Façade of Temple of Apedemak built by King Natakamani and Queen Amanitore. Naga. First Century C.E. Photograph courtesy of Professor S. Sidebotham

Piye, who conquered Egypt about 730 B.C.E. and whose commemorative inscription is the finest extant example of Egyptian historical writing. Thanks to archaeological evidence, historians are now able to also assess more accurately the achievements of later Kushite rulers such as King Natakamani and Queen Amanitore, during whose joint reign in the first century C.E. Kushite culture reached its peak. Nevertheless, historians probably never will be able to write a traditional narrative history of Kush.

The reasons are twofold. First is the lack of native Kushite sources. So, while the number of Meroitic texts has been gradually increasing, historians cannot exploit their evidence, since the Meroitic language still cannot be understood, although the basic principles and sound values of the Meroitic script were established in the early twentieth century. Second, and equally important, the literary sources—Egyptian, Greek, Latin, Assyrian, Hebrew, Axumite, and Syriac—are limited in both number and focus. Most are either descriptions of the geography and customs of Kush or accounts of Kush's relations with Egypt. The reasons for this situation are not in doubt.

Located on the periphery of the Mediterranean world and known primarily as a source of exotic African goods, Greeks treated Kush as an appendage of Egypt, whose history and culture were of interest mainly for the light they threw on Egypt. As a result, historians must rely on archaeological evidence to reconstruct Kushite history. Since archaeological evidence concerns primarily the material culture of a people, it is not surprising that the cultural and not the political history of Kush provides the central theme of modern histories of Kush. Although much remains unclear concerning the details of the history of Kush, one fact is certain: like Egypt, Kush was a gift of the Nile, albeit a less generous and more ambiguous gift.

Outline of Kushite History

The Nile Valley forms a narrow oasis over a thousand miles long that divides the great desert that extends across the whole of North Africa from the Atlantic Ocean to the Red Sea. Its advantages, however, are unequally distributed. The Egyptian Nile has a shallow bed that facilitated the flood that annually renewed the land of Egypt and made Egyptian civilization possible. In contrast, the Sudanese Nile runs through a deep granite-lined channel interrupted by numerous rapids, the famous cataracts, that limits the extent of the flood over much of its course.

As a result, the population of Kush was never more than a small fraction of that of its more powerful northern neighbor. At the same time, the Sudanese Nile, despite the inconveniences caused by the cataracts, provided a corridor through which the traditional products of the trans-Saharan trade—ivory, ebony, incenses, animal products, slaves, and especially gold, for which the Sudan was one of the ancient western world's most important sources—could be easily transported to Egypt, whence they could be distributed throughout the ancient world. These conditions gave rise to a cycle of historical development that recurred throughout most of ancient Kushite history.

Repeatedly, states emerged in Kush and prospered as middlemen in the Nile trade, only to have their existence and development aborted when Egypt exploited her superior power to intervene militarily in the Sudan, subordinate its inhabitants, and seize control of its natural resources and the trade in them. Inevitably, therefore, periods of strong state development and prosperity in Kush tended to coincide with periods of political and military weakness in Egypt, when the Egyptians had to rely on diplomacy and trade to obtain the

African products they desired. Thus, one early Kushite state, whose royal tombs were discovered in the 1960s at Qustul about 150 miles south of the present Aswan high dam, was crushed in the early third millennium B.C.E. by the forces of Old Kingdom Egypt. Again, in the mid-second millennium B.C.E. the imperialist Pharaohs of the eighteenth and nineteenth Egyptian dynasties overwhelmed and colonized the territory of a Kushite kingdom, centered at present day Kerma near the third cataract of the Nile, that had flourished during the first half of the second millennium B.C.E. Only in the first millennium B.C.E. did a fortuitous combination of circumstances free the Kushites from this cruel dilemma and allow their civilization to grow and flourish.

The relocation of the center of Kush first to Napata and then to Meroë deep in the central Sudan, combined with the political collapse of Egypt and its conquest by a series of foreign empires—Assyrian, Persian, Macedonian, and Roman—finally freed the Kushites from the threat of foreign conquest. Indeed, for a brief period in the eighth and early seventh centuries B.C.E., Kushite kings were even able to turn the tables and conquer and rule Egypt (ca. 712–664 B.C.E.). Kushite civilization reached its peak, however, almost seven centuries later. Good relations with the Roman rulers of Egypt and increased demand for the African goods Kush could supply brought unprecedented wealth to its rulers and fostered a great expansion of settlement and construction in the Upper Nile Valley, whose remains are still visible today. Finally, after enduring for over a millennium, Kush succumbed in the fourth century C.E. to a combination of attacks by nomadic peoples from the eastern and western deserts of the Sudan and invasions mounted by the rulers of the recently established kingdom of Axum in present day Ethiopia. The Axumite conquest marked the end

Royal Pyramids. Meroë.
Photograph courtesy of Professor S. Sidebotham.

of Kush, but not of civilization in the Upper Nile Valley. Within a century new kingdoms appeared in the region that would survive for another millennium; but they were ruled by a new people, the Nubians, and based on a new religion, Christianity.

Geography also dictated that Egypt would exercise an important influence on the development of Kushite culture. Some of that influence can be traced to trade. Most, however, was the result of royal initiative. Thus, Egyptian kings pursued an extensive program of colonization and temple building and sought to form a loyal body of Egyptianized Kushite supporters in the second millennium B.C.E. Later Kushite kings also recruited Egyptian craftsmen to work on their monuments. As a result, evidence of Egyptian influence is readily apparent in virtually all areas of Kushite civilization. Obvious examples are: the worship of Egyptian gods such as Isis, Osiris, and Amon; the use of pyramids as royal tombs; the employment of Egyptian artistic conventions in sculpture and architecture; and the use of the Egyptian language and hieroglyphic writing system for the composition of political and religious texts. The Egyptian connection persisted even after the Macedonian and Roman conquest of Egypt, but with two significant differences. First, it was the Kushites who took the initiative in dealing with Egypt; and, second, the influences that flowed south from Egypt included elements of Greek and Roman culture.

Historians' assessments of the significance of these complex influences vary widely, however. The attitudes of early historians of Kush, influenced by the fashionable racism of the nineteenth and early twentieth centuries and the Egyptian denigration of their Kushite neighbors, tended to be negative. In their view Kush was an outpost of superior Egyptian civilization isolated in a hostile and uncreative African environment and condemned, therefore, to slow degeneration. Its positive

Procession of Gods. Royal family paying homage to Apedemak. Temple of Apedemak. Naga. First Century C.E.
Source: K. R. Lepsius, Denkmäler aus Ägypten und Äthiopien (Berlin, 1849–1859) V, 61–62.

role in history was limited to diffusing throughout the rest of Africa cultural innovations borrowed from Egypt such as divine kingship and iron metallurgy. Evaluations by contemporary historians are more positive, emphasizing the Kushites' deliberate selection of Egyptian elements and creative use of them to express local values and realities. Thus, mummification was abandoned in favor of more traditional burial patterns, and Kushite deities such as the lion-headed war god Apedemak gained prominence at the expense of Egyptian gods. Even more revealing, superficially Egyptian artistic creations prove on closer examination to have a distinctively Kushite content. Examples are the prominent role assigned to queens in official art and the accurate depiction of various aspects of local Kushite life and culture, including practices still found among the peoples of the southern Sudan such as facial scarring and the deliberate deformation of the horns of cattle. Nor was Kushite creativity limited to Kush itself.

During the approximately half century they ruled Egypt, the Kushite kings of the Twenty-fifth dynasty reunited the country and sponsored a renaissance of culture that resulted in the creation of some of the greatest works of Egyptian art, and whose effects continued to be felt throughout the remainder of the history of ancient Egypt. They also made Egypt an active and significant player on the international scene again for the first time in almost two centuries and helped delay, albeit only briefly, the conquest by the Assyrians of the smaller peoples of the eastern Mediterranean basin such as the Jews and Phoenicians. Even after their retreat from Egypt, the Kushites continued to influence Egypt in various ways. They protected Egypt's southern border against raids by the nomadic peoples who inhabited the Nubian deserts, while providing Egypt with needed imports from the interior of Africa. Equally important,

Egyptian rebels against foreign rule—Persian and Macedonian —took inspiration from the existence of a powerful independent state in Nubia.

Unfortunately, the full extent of the Kushite achievement will never be fully known. Nor, it must be admitted, were all aspects of that achievement positive. Thus, Kush played a central role in the establishment of the east African slave trade that was only finally abolished in this century. Throughout the whole of antiquity Kush was the principal source of African slaves for the civilizations of the ancient Mediterranean world. Her successor states continued to be important suppliers of slaves to Egypt and the Near East in the Medieval and early modern periods. Only the conquest of the Sudan in the nineteenth century, first by Egypt and then by Britain, ended that role.

AXUM

As already noted, the ultimate fate of Kush was intimately connected with the rise of another ancient African state, that of Axum, in the highlands of the province of Tigray in the northeastern portion of modern Ethiopia. Unlike Kush, Axum is the name not of a state but of a city that became first the political capital of a powerful empire, and then the principal religious center of the oldest Christian state on the African continent. At the height of their power, the kings of Axum ruled an empire that extended from the Upper Nile Valley in the west to Yemen in the East and was considered together with Rome, Persia, and China one of the four great empires that divided ancient Eurasia and Africa between them. Even after its abandonment as the political capital of Ethiopia in the eighth century C.E., Axum continued to be venerated as the cultural and religious center of Ethiopia. As late as the twentieth century Ethiopian kings were crowned amidst the ruins of ancient Axum, and people from all over Ethiopia made pilgrimages to the cathedral of Mary of Zion to venerate the most holy relic of Ethiopian Christianity, the Ark of the Covenant, which tradition held had been miraculously brought to Ethiopia from Jerusalem after the sack of the city by the Romans in 70 C.E.

The Historiography of Axum

Unlike Kush, Axum has a rich native literary tradition. Unfortunately, this literature is of little use to historians interested in reconstructing the history of ancient Axum. The reason is clear. From the thirteenth century C.E. to the 1970s Ethiopia was ruled by kings of the so-called Solomonic dynasty who claimed to be descendants of Menelek, the son of King Solomon and the Queen of Sheba. Axum played a critical role in the ideology of the Solomonic dynasty because it was believed to have been the home of the Queen of Sheba, where Menelek's descendants ruled until they were driven into exile by usurpers in the early Middle Ages.[4] Because of the heavy ideological burden of the native literary tradition concerning Axum, historians must rely on other sources to reconstruct Axumite history, and, fortunately, a wide variety of such sources exist. These sources include: (1) Axumite royal inscriptions and coins, (2) references to Axum in ancient Classical and Christian literature, (3) European travelers' reports, and (4) modern archaeology.

The most important of these sources are the Axumite royal inscriptions and coins. Axumite kings routinely set up monumental inscriptions in Greek and two Semitic languages—Ge'ez and Sabaean—to commemorate their victories, and many of these inscriptions survive. In addition, they issued an important coinage—the earliest native African coinage—which

Coin of Aphilas (Fourth Century C.E.*). Pagan crescent and disk symbols.*
Greek Inscription: Aphilas King of the Axumites, Man of Dimele.

Coin of Armah (Seventh Century C.E.*). Cross. Ge'ez Inscription:*
King Armah. May he be a joy to the people.
Source: Enno Littmann, Deutsche Aksum-Expedition
(Berlin, 1913) I, 46 and 56.

often provides important evidence for the existence of kings mentioned nowhere else in the sources. In addition, Axum is frequently mentioned in Classical and Christian literature because of the important role it played in late Roman and early Byzantine policy in southern Arabia.

After Axum ceased to be the royal capital in the early Middle Ages, the city fell into ruin. Serious archaeological exploration of the ruins of Axum began only in the twentieth century, and by then much of the ancient city had disappeared. Fortunately, a long line of European travelers and explorers—beginning with Italian and Portuguese emissaries and missionaries in the Renaissance and including the great 18th century Scottish explorer James Bruce—described many Axumite monuments that are no longer extant. On the basis of these varied sources historians have reconstructed the outlines of the history of one of the greatest African states.

Outline of Axumite History

Although the first signs of state formation in the territory of modern Ethiopia date from the third millennium B.C.E., the roots of the Axumite state lie in the early first millennium B.C.E. when colonists from South Arabia crossed the Red Sea and settled in Eritrea and Tigray. Sabaean inscriptions and monumental architecture and sculpture attest to the emergence of several tribal kingdoms in the region before the ruler of one of them, that of the Habasha (=Abyssinians), chose the site of Axum as his capital most likely sometime in the last centuries B.C.E., since it is attested as a royal capital in the first century C.E. The choice was an astute one.

Located high on the Ethiopian plateau with easy access to the upper Nile Valley and its hinterlands on the west and to the Red Sea on the east through the nearby port of Adulis, Axum was ideally situated to profit from its position astride the trade routes that linked the Mediterranean to Northeast Africa, South Arabia, and the Indian Ocean. Already in the second half of the first century C.E. *The Periplus of the Erythraean Sea* reveals Axum to be the chief commercial center of the Southern Red Sea basin. The fact that its ruler is described as literate in Greek attests to the existence already of close ties between Axum and Roman Egypt. Although direct evidence is lacking, Axumite power grew rapidly. By the mid-third century C.E. Axum had acquired an empire that included most of modern Ethiopia and Eritrea as well as important parts of southern Arabia and had displaced Kush as the principal supplier of African goods to Rome. With the conquest of Meroë in the mid-fourth century C.E., Axumite territory reached its maximum extent.

Little is known about how the Axumites governed their empire. Axumite kings styled themselves "King of Kings" and listed numerous peoples they claimed to rule in their titularies. Combined with references to various local rulers in their inscriptions, this has suggested to scholars that the Axumite empire had a "federal" structure in which the King of Axum and his family controlled the central government and military while leaving local regions in the hands of their traditional ruling families. References to local rebellions in the sources highlight the difficulties of controlling such a vast and decentralized state, and by the early sixth century C.E. Axum had lost its frontier provinces in the Nile Valley and South Arabia. Control of its Ethiopian and Eritrean core remained firm, and its conversion to Christianity in the mid-fourth century C.E. made Axum the principal guardian of Rome's southern flank in its bitter wars with Persia in the early sixth century C.E. Axumite prosperity depended, however, on its key role in the lucrative Red Sea and Indian Ocean trade. The disruption of that trade by the Arab conquest of Egypt and the Near East sapped

Stela. Axum.
Photograph courtesy of Professor David W. Phillipson.

Axum's prosperity and resulted in the gradual decline and ultimate abandonment of the city, as its last kings moved their capital to a more defensible site in the interior of Ethiopia.

For over half a millennium Axum flourished, producing a rich culture that created in the great stelae of Axum some of the spectacular monuments of the ancient world. Unfortunately, little is known about other aspects of Axumite culture. Christianity has been the dominant religion of Ethiopia since the mid-fourth century C.E., and, as happened elsewhere, conversion to Christianity was followed by repudiation of many of the former traditions of Axum. So, although the existence of the Ge'ez translation of the Bible and the trilingual royal inscriptions clearly indicate that pre-Christian Axum had a literary tradition, no Axumite literature survives. The same is also true for Axumite art. As a result, historians have to rely on the extant inscriptions and monuments for the little we know about Axumite culture.

These sources indicate that Axumite culture was a blend of African, Mediterranean, and southern Arabian traditions in which the South Arabian strand was dominant. Thus, the official language of Axum was Ge'ez, a Semitic language, which was written in an alphabetic script derived from South Arabia. Axumite architecture followed South Arabian models and the kings of Axum applied South Arabian hydraulic engineering techniques to ensure a reliable water supply for Axum. The Axumites also worshipped South Arabian gods. The most important of these gods was Mahrem, the war-god, who was reputed to be the ancestor of the kings and their helper in battle. Unfortunately, it is not possible to go beyond this bare sketch at present. Presumably, much Axumite tradition survives in the Christian culture of Medieval and Modern Ethiopia, but only the discovery of new evidence will allow us to identify such survivals with certainty.

PLAN OF THE BOOK

The thousand years of history treated in this book not only represent the peak of civilization in ancient Nubia and Ethiopia, but they are also the best documented. Although limited in number, the sources are varied and include geographic and ethnographic texts, secular and church histories, private and public inscriptions, and commercial documents. Despite occasional distortion resulting from ethnocentrism and the familiar tendency of travelers to privilege the bizarre over the routine, these texts provide valuable evidence for many otherwise undocumented aspects of life in ancient Northeast Africa including: religious ritual, trade, social and political institutions, foreign relations, warfare, and even personal piety. Translations of the most important of these documents are included in this book either in revised versions or in new ones made especially for it.[5] Each document is accompanied by brief explanatory notes and an introduction that identifies its origin and basic characteristics and places it in historical context. As a result, teachers and students of African and World History now will have at their disposal a source book for ancient Kushite and Axumite history. Hopefully, this also will encourage the study of the history of two of the least known but most interesting civilizations of the ancient world.

I

KUSH AND ITS NEIGHBORS

1.

THE EXPLORATION OF NUBIA
AND THE RED SEA

Although Egyptian expeditions penetrated deep into the Sudan as early as the third millennium B.C.E., *the Egyptians never developed a tradition of collecting and preserving in written form information concerning the ethnography of the region. In the following passage the late first century* B.C.E. *geographer Strabo summarizes Greek views concerning the history of Nubian exploration and the critical role of the early Ptolemies in expanding knowledge of the region.*

The ancients understood more by conjecture than otherwise, but people in later times learned by experience as eyewitnesses, that the Nile owes its rise to summer rains. These fall in great abundance in Upper Aithiopia, particularly in the most distant mountains. When the rains cease, the flood gradually subsides. This was particularly observed by those who navigated the Arabian Gulf on their way to the Cinnamon country,[1] and by those the Ptolemaic kings of Egypt sent out to hunt elephants or dispatched to that region for other reasons. These kings were interested in such activities, particularly Ptolemy, surnamed Philadelphus (282–246 B.C.E.), who was a lover of science, and always seeking some new diversion or amusement because of bodily infirmities.

But the ancient kings of Egypt paid little attention to such inquiries, although they and the priests, with whom they passed the greater part of their lives, professed to be devoted to the study of philosophy. Their ignorance, therefore, is more surprising, both for this reason and because Sesostris[2] had traversed the whole of Aithiopia as far as the Cinnamon country. Monuments of his campaign including pillars and inscriptions are pointed out still today. Cambyses also, when he was in possession of Egypt, advanced with the Egyptians as far even as Meroë.[3] People say that he gave this name both to the island and to the city, because his sister, or, according to some, his wife, Meroë, died there. He gave the name to the island, therefore, in order to honor this woman.

Further information about the role played by attempts to solve the problem of Nile Flood in the expansion of Greek knowledge of Nubia is provided by the late first century B.C.E. universal historian Diodorus of Argyrium.

The Nile flood was the source of great dispute. Many philosophers and historians tried to explain the cause of this phenomenon. With regard to the rise of the Nile and its sources, and its exits to the sea and the other ways in which it differs from other rivers, it being the largest in the inhabited world, some writers simply did not dare to say anything, although they were accustomed at times to write at length about some stream. Others attempted to discuss the problems but totally missed the truth.

Hellanicus, Cadmus, Hecataeus,[4] and all other such individuals, who wrote in very early times, inclined toward mythical explanations. Herodotus, who was an ardent seeker after knowledge if ever there was one, and well informed about history, attempted to provide an account of these matters. His theories, however, have been found to be contradictory.

Xenophon and Thucydides, who are praised for the accuracy of their histories, refrained entirely from discussing places beyond Egypt. Ephorus and Theopompus,[5] who of all writers concerned themselves with these subjects, were furthest from the truth.

All of these writers failed not because of lack of diligence but because of the peculiar characteristics of the country. From ancient times until the reign of Ptolemy Philadelphus Greeks not only did not cross into Aithiopia, but they did not even travel as far as the borders of Egypt. Conditions in these regions were completely hostile to foreigners and extremely dangerous. Ptolemy Philadelphus, however, was the first to campaign in Aithiopia with a Greek army and from his time that country has become more accurately known.[6] Such, therefore, were the reasons for the ignorance of earlier writers.

With regard to the sources of the Nile and the place where the river originates, no historian up to the present has said anything or revealed knowledge learned from those who clearly had seen it. For this reason the subject has become a matter for surmise and plausible speculation. The Egyptian priests declare that its source is in the Ocean that flows around the inhabited world.[7] In saying this, however, they do not advance a sound position, as they try to resolve a problem with something problematic, basing on faith a theory that requires much faith. Those of the Trogodytes[8] who have moved from the southern regions because of the heat and are called Bolgioi, report certain facts about these places which would lead one to conclude the main stream of the Nile is built from many sources which collect together in one place. This is the reason that the Nile is the most fertile of all known rivers. On the other hand, the inhabitants of the island of Meroë, with whom one would be particularly included to agree since they are strongly averse to plausible speculation and live nearest the regions in question, are so hesitant to say anything precise about these issues that they call the river the "Astapous" which translated into Greek means "water from the shadows."[9] They, therefore, assign to the Nile an appellation appropriate to the lack of reliable observations concerning these areas and their own ignorance.

2

A GREEK ACCOUNT OF THE GEOGRAPHY OF NUBIA

The period of peak Greek involvement in Nubia was relatively brief, extending for less than a century from the late 270s B.C.E. to the end of the third century B.C.E. During that short period, however, Greek contact with Nubia was intense. That contact took many forms, including not only military and diplomatic encounters between Ptolemaic Egypt and the kingdom of Meroë, but also repeated incursions into Meroitic territory by Ptolemaic hunting expeditions seeking elephants to capture and bring back to Egypt for training as war elephants. An important by-product of these activities was a great increase in the precision and detail of Greek knowledge of Nubia that is reflected in the accurate description of the geography of the Upper Nile valley by the third century B.C.E. geographer Eratosthenes of Cyrene that is translated below.

Eratosthenes says that the Nile lies 1000 stades west of the Arabian Gulf.[10] The Nile resembles in its course the letter N reversed. For after flowing, he says, about 2700 stades from Meroë towards the north, it turns again to the south, and to the winter sunset, continuing its course for about 3700 stades, when it is almost in the latitude of the places about Meroë. Then after entering deep into Libya,[11] and having made another bend, it flows towards the north, a distance of 5300 stades, to the great cataract. Finally, after turning a little to the east, it traverses a distance of 1200 stades to the smaller cataract at Syene, and then 5300 stades more to the sea.

Two rivers empty into the Nile. These flow out of some lakes towards the east, and encircle Meroë, a considerable island. One of these rivers is called Astaboras and flows along the eastern side of the island.[12] The other is the Astapous, or, as some call it, Astasobas. But the Astapous is said to be another river, which flows out of some lakes on the south. This river forms almost the whole of the main body of the Nile, which flows in a straight line.[13] The Nile is filled by the summer rains.[14] Above the junction of the Astaboras and the Nile, at the distance of 700 stades, lies Meroë, a city having the same name as the island. There is also another island above Meroë, occupied by the fugitive Egyptians who revolted in the time of Psammetichus and are called Sembritae, or foreigners.[15] Their sovereign is a queen, but they obey the king of Meroë.

The lower parts of the country on each side of Meroë, along the Nile towards the Red Sea, are occupied by Megabari and Blemmyes.[16] These peoples are subject to the Aithiopians, and border upon the Egyptians. The Trogodytes live near the sea.[17] The Trogodytes, in the latitude of Meroë, are distant ten or twelve days' journey from the Nile. On the left of the course of the Nile live Nubae[18] in Libya, a populous nation. They begin from Meroë, and extend as far as the bends of the Nile. They are not subject to the Aithiopians, but live independently, being divided into several tribes.

3.

The Gold Mines of Lower Nubia

Gold, the "Flesh of the Gods" as the Egyptians called it, has always been one of the most sought-after products of Nubia. Nubian gold made New Kingdom Egypt the wealthiest state in the Ancient Near East. Although gold deposits can be found throughout the Upper Nile valley, the most productive mines were located in a series of dry river beds—called wadis in Arabic—in the deserts east of the Nile in Lower Nubia. Even today, abandoned mine shafts, gold processing equipment, and the ruins of ancient mining settlements are among the most common remains of ancient life in the deserts of southern Egypt and the northern Sudan. Control of one of the most important of these gold mining regions, the Wadi Allaqi, was one of the most significant gains made by the Ptolemies in their encounters with Kush in the third century B.C.E.; and Nubian gold helped finance the foreign policy initiatives in the Mediterranean basin of these ambitious Macedonian rulers of Egypt. The horrific conditions under which criminals and political prisoners labored to wrest the "Flesh of the Gods" from the soil of Nubia are vividly described by the second B.C.E. historian Agatharchides of Cnidus in this selection from his On the Erythraean Sea.

Near the furthest point of Egypt and the neighboring regions of Arabia and Aithiopia there is a place that has many large gold mines.[19] There much gold is collected with great suffering and expense. The land is naturally black with seams and veins of quartz that are remarkable for their whiteness and surpass all stones that shine brilliantly. Those in charge of the mining obtain the gold with a multitude of workers.

For the kings of Egypt[20] collect together and consign to the gold mines those condemned for crimes and prisoners of war, and in addition, those who have been the victims of unjust accusations and sent to prison because of their wrath, sometimes themselves alone and sometimes together with their whole families. Thus, at the same time, they exact punishment from those condemned and obtain great revenues from their labor. Those convicts, who are numerous and bound with fetters, work at their tasks continuously during the day and throughout the whole night, being allowed no respite at all and rigorously prevented from all possibility of escape. For barbarian soldiers, who speak different languages, are appointed to be guards so that the prisoners cannot corrupt any of their warders through human conversation or some human appeal.

They pursue their task in the mountains where the gold is found. They light wood fires on the stone outcrops, which are jagged and extremely hard, and crumble them with the heat.[21]

Having heated the hardest part of the earth which contains the gold and broken it into small pieces, they carry on their work with their hands. Tens of thousands of unfortunate men crush with iron sledges the rock that has been fragmented and can be broken up with little effort. A technician, who evaluates the rock, is in charge of the whole process and gives assignments to the workers. Of those sentenced to this misery, the men distinguished by their bodily strength break up the quartz rock with iron hammers, not by applying skill to their tasks but by brute force. They also excavate galleries, not in a straight line but whichever way goes the vein of the gleaming rock.

As they work in darkness because of the twists and turns of the galleries, these men wear lamps fastened on their foreheads. Often forcing their bodies to conform to the peculiarities of the rock, they throw down on the floor the fragments they have quarried. They do this continuously in response to the brutality and blows of the overseers.

Young boys, who go down through the galleries to the areas of rock that have been excavated, laboriously pick up the rock that is being dug out bit by bit and carry it outside to a place near the entrance. Men over thirty years of age take it from them and pound a fixed amount of the quarried rock on stone mortars with iron pestles until they reduce it to the size of a vetch seed. The women and older men receive from them the seed sized rock and cast it into stone mills, several of which stand in a line; and standing beside them, two or three to a handle, they grind it until they reduce the portion given them to a flour-like state. Since there is general neglect of their bodies and they have no garment to cover their shame, it is impossible for an observer to not pity the wretches because of the extremity of their suffering. For they meet with no respite at all, not the sick, the injured, the aged, not a woman by reason of her weakness, but all are compelled by blows to strive at their tasks until, exhausted by the abuse they suffered, they die in their miseries. For this reason the poor wretches think that the future always will be more fearful than the present because of the extreme severity of their punishment, and they consider death more desirable than life.

Finally, the technicians, after collecting the ground-up rock, bring the process to its final conclusion. For they rub the processed quartz on a flat slightly inclined board while pouring on water. Then the earthy portion which has been flushed out by the water flows away following the inclination of the board, but the part that contains the gold remains behind on the wood because of its weight. Doing this repeatedly, they at first rub it lightly with their hand, and later washing it with porous sponges, they skim off with these the loose and earthy portions until only the pure particles of gold remain.

Finally, other technicians gather up the gold that has collected, and pack it according to a fixed measure and weight into pottery vessels. They mix in a lump of lead of a size proportionate to the amount of gold and pieces of salt and, in addition, they add a little tin and barley bran. Having covered it with a close fitting lid and thoroughly sealed it with clay, they bake it in a kiln for five days and an equal number of nights continuously. Then, after allowing it to cool, they find in the jars none of the other substances, but they obtain pure gold with only a small amount having been lost.

The death of numerous men in the mines brings our exposition to the conclusion already stated, namely, that, as its nature clearly demonstrates, the origin of gold is laborious, its preservation is uncertain, it is most zealously sought after, and its use lies between pleasure and pain. Further, the manner in which it is mined is extremely ancient. For the nature of the mines was discovered by the first rulers of the region, but their working was suspended when the Aithiopians...invaded Egypt in force and garrisoned its cities for many years and (again) during the supremacy of the Medes and Persians.[22] Even in our time bronze chisels are found in the gold mines excavated by those rulers because the use of iron was not yet known at that time. Human bones in unbelievable numbers are also found since, as was likely to have happened, many cave-ins occurred in the unstable galleries with their brittle walls, given the great extent of the excavations and their reaching in their deepest sections the sea itself.

4.

A Description of Meroë

The annexation of the gold mining regions of northern Nubia enriched the Ptolemies. The center of Kushite civilization, however, lay far to south, below the fifth cataract of the Nile in the famous "Island of Meroë" in the central Sudan. Although Herodotus, the father of History, had already heard of Meroë, the last and greatest capital of Kush, in the fifth century B.C.E., accurate knowledge concerning Meroë only became current in the Greek world in the third century B.C.E., when Ptolemaic explorers and diplomats visited the city and described it and its environs. From then until the end of antiquity, Meroë served as one of the fundamental reference points of Greek world geography, being the southernmost of the seven cities, whose latitudes Greek geographers used to define the limits of the "oecumene": the civilized world.

In Aithiopia there are many islands.[23] One, which is named Meroë, is very large and has on it a notable city of the same name. The city was founded by Cambyses, who named it after his mother Meroë. They say that this island is similar in shape to an oblong shield and that it is far greater in size than the other islands in these regions. Its length is said to be three thousand stades and its breadth one thousand stades. This island contains not a few cities, of which Meroë is the most distinguished. <In the cities houses are made of split pieces of

palm wood that are woven together or of brick.> The island, which is everywhere bathed by water, is bordered on the Libyan side by enormous sand dunes and on the Arabian side by rugged cliffs. <Above, from the south, it is bounded by the junctions of the rivers Astaboras, Astapous, and Astasobas while toward the north its boundary is created by the next stretch of the Nile, which extends to Egypt and passes through the bends of the river.>[24] The island also contains <many mountains and dense thickets. Nomads, hunters, farmers inhabit it.> There are on it also gold, silver, and copper mines, as well as an abundance of <trees including palm, Persea,> ebony, <and Ceratia>, as well as every sort of precious stone. <Its inhabitants also have quarried salt just like the Arabs. Above Meroë lies Psebo, a large lake containing a relatively well-populated island.>[25] Speaking generally, the river makes so many islands that people easily believe what they hear. Apart from the places embraced in the so-called Delta, there are more than seven hundred other islands. Those which are irrigated by the Aithiopians grow millet. Others are full of snakes, baboons, and all sorts of other wild animals and cannot for that reason be approached by men.

5.

The History and Customs of the People of Kush

Ptolemaic agents also provided Greek readers with their first detailed accounts of the ethnography of Kush. We know the names of seven writers of Aithiopika *(works about Kush), one of whom, Simonides the Younger, claimed to have lived in Meroë for five years. Although these works are lost, a summary of their main findings is preserved in the following passage, which served as the main source of information about Hellenistic Kush until archaeological exploration of the principal sites of Meroitic civilization in the nineteenth and twentieth centuries* C.E. *enabled historians to propose reconstructions of the history of Kush on the basis of native sources. These new sources have confirmed the accuracy of much of the information contained in this passage, such as the close relationship between Kushite and Pharaonic Egyptian culture. They have also revealed, however, that this information is embedded in a matrix of historical and ethnographic theories that often reflects Greek rather than Kushite ideas.*

Historians record that the Aithiopians were the first of all men, and they say that the proofs of this proposition are clear and manifest. For it is agreed by almost everyone that the Aithiopians are properly called *autochthones*, since they did not

Stela of King Tanyidamani. Napata. Second Century B.C.E. King paying homage to Amon and Isis. Inscription in Meroitic script. Photograph courtesy of Museum of Fine Arts, Boston.

enter their land as foreigners but were natives of it. That it is plausible that those living in the south were the first to be given life by the earth is also clear to everyone. Since the heat of the sun dried out the earth which was still moist and life bearing when everything came into existence, it is likely that the place nearest the sun would first bring forth animate beings.

Historians also say that the honoring of gods and the conducting of sacrifices, processions, festivals, and the other ways by which men worship the divine first were introduced among the Aithiopians. For this reason their piety has become famous among all men, and the sacrifices performed by the Aithiopians are believed to be particularly agreeable to the divine power. They offer as a witness to these facts the poet who is virtually the oldest and most admired among the Greeks. For in the *Iliad* (1.423–424) this poet (Homer) introduces Zeus and the other gods as going to Aithiopia each year for the sacrifices established for them and to share a common feast with the Aithiopians themselves.

For yesterday Zeus went to Ocean to the blameless Aithiopians
for a feast, and all the other gods followed him.

They also say that their reverence for the divine clearly brought them advantages, since they never experienced foreign rule. For they have remained in freedom and harmony with each other from the beginning of time. Many powerful enemies have marched against them, but none has met with success.

Cambyses[26] attacked them with a great force and lost his whole army and even risked losing his own life with everything. Likewise, Semiramis,[27] who is famed for the magnitude of her undertakings and deeds, advanced only a short distance into Aithiopia and then gave up her campaign against the whole people. As for Heracles and Dionysus, who marched throughout the whole inhabited world, they only failed to subdue the Aithiopians, who live south of Egypt, because of the piety of these men and the extreme difficulty of the undertaking.

The Aithiopians say,[28] however, that the Egyptians are their colonists and that Osiris was the leader of the colony. For they say that in general what is now Egypt was not land but sea at the time the world was originally created. But later as mud brought down from Aithiopia by the Nile was deposited at the time of the flood, the land gradually advanced. The strongest proof that their land is wholly the result of deposition by the river is provided by what happens at the outlets of the Nile. Each year as new mud continually collects at the mouths of the river, the sea is seen to be pushed back by the mounds, and the land increases. Most of the customs of the Egyptians are also Aithiopian, the colonists having preserved their ancient practices. Believing their kings to be gods, taking particular care with regard to their tombs, and many other similar practices are all Aithiopian customs. The forms of their statues and the shapes of their letters are also Aithiopian. The Egyptians possess two distinct writing systems. One which is called "popular" everyone learns and the other which is called "sacred" by the Egyptians, the priests alone know, having learned it secretly from their fathers. Among the Aithiopians, however, everyone uses these latter forms.[29] The class of priests is similarly organized among both peoples. All those engaged in the worship of the gods purify themselves, shaving themselves in a similar manner, wearing the same robes, and possessing a scepter shaped like a plow,[30] which the kings also have and use. The kings also wear large felt hats with a knob on the top[31] and encircled by snakes which they call asps.[32] This seems intended to be a sign that those who dare to attack the king will meet with fatal bites. The Aithiopians recount many other things about their own antiquity and the Egyptian colony, which it would be of no benefit to record.

Not a few of the customs of the Aithiopians differ greatly from those of other peoples. This is particularly true of their manner of choosing their kings. The priests make a preliminary selection from their own number of the best persons. Whomever of those thus selected is picked out by the god[33] while he is carried about in accordance with a certain custom during a festival, this person the people choose to be king. The people then immediately prostrate themselves and honor him like a god on the ground that the rule had been entrusted to him by divine providence.[34] The person so chosen follows a way of life determined by the laws, and in other matters acts in accordance with ancestral custom, assigning neither benefit nor punishment to anyone contrary to the custom that has been established among them since their origin. It is their custom that none of his subjects are to be executed, even if the person condemned to death appears to deserve punishment. Instead the king sends one of his servants bearing a symbol of death to the criminal. He upon seeing the symbol, immediately goes to his own house and kills himself. It is in no way permissible for a person to flee from his own country into a neighboring land and by the change of country cancel the penalty as is done among the Greeks. They also say that it was for this reason that one person, to whom the fatal sign had been sent by the king and who planned to flee from Aithiopia but whose mother on perceiving his plan strangled him with her girdle, did not dare to lay hands on her at all, but endured being strangled until he died lest he leave behind a greater shame to his kinsmen.

The strangest of all their customs, however, is that concerning the death of their kings. In Meroë, whenever it enters the mind of the priests, who care for the worship and rites of the gods and occupy the highest and most exalted status, they send a messenger to the king ordering him to die. They say that the gods have revealed this to them and that the order of the immortals must in no way be disregarded by those of mortal nature. They also assert other things such as would be accepted by a nature of limited intelligence that has been raised in accordance with customs that are ancient and difficult to eradicate and does not possess arguments with which to oppose arbitrary commands. In earlier times, therefore, the kings obeyed the priests, not having been conquered by weapons or force but their reason having been overcome by this superstition. During the reign of the second Ptolemy (285–246 B.C.E.), however, Ergamenes,[35] the king of the Aithiopians, who had received a Greek education and understood philosophy, first dared to spurn this practice. He made a decision that was worthy of his royal rank and entered accompanied by some soldiers the shrine where was located the gold temple of the Aithiopians, and killed all the priests. After abolishing this custom, he reorganized affairs in accordance with his own plans.

As for the custom concerning the friends of the king, although it is incredible, people say that it remains in force in our time. They say that the Aithiopians have the custom that, whenever the king is wounded in some part of his body for whatever reason, all his companions freely choose to lose that same part. They believe that it would be shameful if the king was lame and his friends were sound of foot and did not all accompany him on his excursions similarly lame. For it would be strange if true friendship joins in mourning and grief and similarly shares in all other goods and ills, but would have no part of bodily harm. They say that it is also customary for their companions to be willing to die with the kings. They also say that this form of death is glorious and evidence of true friendship. For this reason, they say that it is difficult among the Aithiopians to plot against the king, since all his friends consider that his and their safety are on an equal level. These, therefore, are the customs of the Aithiopians who inhabit their capital and occupy the island of Meroë and the country neighboring Egypt.[36]

There are also numerous other tribes of Aithiopians. Some of these occupy the areas along both sides of the Nile and the islands in the river. Others inhabit the neighboring regions of Arabia[37] and the interior of Libya. Most of these tribes, and especially those living along the river, are black in color and have flat faces and curly hair. They are completely wild in their souls and manifest their beastliness not so much in their characters as in their practices. Every aspect of their bodies is squalid. They have extremely long nails similar to wild animals and are almost totally lacking in humane feelings toward each other. Since they speak in high pitched tones and possess none of the practices characteristic of civilized life that are found among other peoples, their customs differ greatly from ours.

Some arm themselves with shields of untanned oxhide and small spears, and some with javelins without throwing straps. Sometimes they employ wooden bows that are four cubits in length which they shoot while bracing them with their foot. When they have exhausted their arrows, they finish the battle with wooden clubs. They also arm their women and set a specific age for their service. Most of these tribes also have the custom of their women wearing a bronze ring in their lip. Some do not wear clothes at all, going about always naked and employing simple types of protection which they obtain from their environment. Some cut off the tails and end of the hides of their cattle and use them to conceal their genitals, hiding them as though shameful. Some wear the skins of domesticated animals, and some cover their bodies to the waist with aprons woven from hair, perhaps because their flocks do not bear wool because of the peculiar conditions of their country. <The Aithiopians live on millet and barley, from which they make a drink. Instead of olive oil they have butter and fat. They have no fruit trees except for a few date-palms in the royal gardens.>[38] For sustenance some of the other tribes collect fruit that is found in the water and which grows naturally in lakes and marshes. Some break off the tips of the thinnest branches and by using these to shade themselves at mid-day, they cool themselves. There are some that plant sesame and lotus and some that rely on the tenderest roots of reeds. Not a few of them develop through practice skill with their bows and accurately shoot many birds, by means of which they satisfy their natural needs. Most, however, rely for their whole life on meat, <blood>, milk, and cheese which they obtain from their herds.[39]

Concerning the gods, those who live above Meroë hold two opinions. They believe that some of the gods have an eternal and incorruptible nature such as the sun and moon and the whole universe, and some they think had had a mortal nature but because of their excellence and their common benefactions toward men they have received immortal honors. They worship Isis and Pan, and also Heracles and Zeus,[40] believing that the human race had received particular benefit from these. A few of the Aithiopians, however, do not believe that there are gods at all. For this reason they curse the sun as their worst enemy when it rises in the east, and flee to the marshes.

They also follow strange customs with regard to their dead. Some throw the bodies into the river and let them go in the belief that this is the finest grave. Others coat the bodies in glass and preserve them in their homes, believing that the visage of those who have died ought not to be unknown to their kin nor that those related by family ties should be forgotten by their relatives. Some, however, place the bodies in terra-cotta coffins and bury them around their temples, and they consider an oath sworn upon these to be the most weighty oath.

As for kingship, some of them entrust it to the handsomest men in the belief that sole rule and good looks are both gifts of fortune. Others select as rulers those who exercise the most care in the maintenance of their flocks on the grounds that they alone will take most thought for their subjects. Some assign this office to the wealthiest, thinking that only these will be able to care for people because of the availability of their wealth. There are also, however, some who choose as their kings those who are distinguished for courage, judging that those who excel in war are alone worthy of leadership.

There is a certain portion of the territory along the Nile in Libya that is distinguished for its beauty. It bears abundant and varied food and provides effective protection against excessive heat in refuges in the marshes. This place is contested by the Libyans and the Aithiopians, and they fight continually with each other over it. Moreover, numerous elephants enter it from the upper country, as some say, because of the abundance and delightfulness of the pasturage. Marshes extend along the banks of the river, and abundant food of all sorts grow in these places. Wherefore, when they get a taste of the rushes and reeds, the elephants remain and destroy the property of the men. For this reason, the people, who are nomads and tent dwellers and generally define their territories according to their convenience, are compelled to take refuge in these places. The herds of elephants leave the country in the interior because everything that grows in that region quickly withers. The pasturage is dry and scarce because of the excessive heat and the lack of spring and river water. Some say, however, that snakes that are remarkable for their size and number are found in what is called the "wild country." These snakes attack the elephants near water sources. As they struggle with the elephants, they wrap their coils around their legs, and they continue applying force and crushing them with these bonds until finally the beasts, drenched in sweat, collapse under the burden. Then the snakes gather together and consume the fallen animal, easily overcoming the beast because of its inability to move.[41] A puzzle remains, namely, why the snakes do not pursue the elephants into the land by the river when they seek their accustomed food. People say that the great snakes avoid the flat land and live permanently in the ravines that extend to great length near the foothills and in deep caverns. For this reason they never leave the places that are advantageous and familiar to them, since nature provides instinctive guidance in such matters to all creatures. Such is what we have to say concerning the Aithiopians and their country.

6.

The Trogodytes: Nomads of the Nubian Desert

The interest of Ptolemaic officials and Greek historians centered on the civilized inhabitants of the Island of Meroë. In the deserts and mountains east of the Nile, however, lived other peoples, the various nomadic tribes Greeks referred to collectively as "Trogodytes." The meaning of the term "Trogodytes" is unknown, but like their descendants, the Beja tribes of the medieval and modern Sudan, their livelihood was dependent on their flocks of sheep and herds of cattle. Also like the Beja, the Trogodytes were formidable warriors, whose raids threatened settled populations and travelers alike. The Napatan predecessors of the kings of Meroë repeatedly refer in their inscriptions to their struggles with the peoples of the deserts, while the shrine of Pan Euodos, "Pan of the Good Road," at el-Kaneis in Egypt contains numerous dedications by grateful Ptolemaic travelers who had been "saved from the Trogodytes."

Now, the Trogodytes[42] are called "Nomads" by the Greeks and live a wandering life supported by their herds in groups ruled by tyrants.[43] Together with their children they have their women in common except for the one belonging to the tyrant. Against a person who has sexual relations with her the chief levies as a fine a specified number of sheep.

This is their way of life.[44] When it is winter in their country—this is at the time of the Etesian winds[45]—and the god inundates their land with heavy rains, they draw their sustenance from blood and milk, which they mix together and stir in jars which have been slightly heated. When summer comes, however, they live in the marshlands, fighting among themselves over the pasture. They eat those of their animals that are old and sick after they have been slaughtered by butchers whom they call "Unclean."

They do not assign to any human being the appellation "parent" but to a bull and a cow, calling the former "father" and the latter "mother" and likewise to a ram and a ewe because they do not obtain their daily sustenance from their parents but from these beasts. For drink the mass of the people employs a preparation made from the Christ's thorn plant, but the tyrants drink one that is prepared from a particular flower and is like poor quality sweet wine. They leave the rest of their body naked but cover their loins with a girdle of skins. It is customary for the other Trogodytes to circumcise their genital organs, just as do the Egyptians, but the tribe the Greeks call "Colobi" have the custom of cutting off with razors during infancy the whole portion that others circumcise. From this practice they gained for themselves the appellation just mentioned.[46]

For armament the tribe of Trogodytes called Megabari have circular shields made of raw ox-hide and clubs tipped with iron knobs, but the others have bows and spears.

He says that the Trogodytes deal as follows with the dead. With withies made from the Christ's thorn plant they bind the neck to the legs. Then, after they place the body on a mound, they pelt it with stones large enough to be held in a hand while jeering and laughing until they have hidden the corpse. They then place on top (of the cairn) the horn of a goat and depart free of sadness and completely cheerful. In conducting this sort of funeral, he says, they act sensibly since to not cause themselves grief on account of those who are free from pain is a sign of intelligence.

They do not fight with each other, as the Greeks do, over land or some other pretext but over the pasturage as it sprouts up at various times. In their feuds, they first pelt each other with stones until some are wounded. Then for the remainder of the battle they resort to a contest of bows and arrows. In a short time many die as they shoot accurately because of their practice in this pursuit and their aiming at a target bare of defensive weapons. The older women, however, put an end to the battle by rushing in between them and meeting with respect. For it is their custom not to strike these women on any account so that immediately upon their appearance the men cease shooting.

They do not, he says, sleep as do other men. They possess a large number of animals which accompany them, and they hang cowbells from the horns of all the males in order that their sound might drive off wild beasts. At nightfall, they collect their herds into byres and cover these with hurdles made from palm branches. Their women and children mount up on top of these. The men, however, light fires in a circle and sing traditional tales and thus ward off sleep, since in many situations discipline imposed by nature is able to conquer nature.

Those individuals who are unable to follow the herds because of age wind the tail of a cow around their necks and willingly free themselves from life. But should one seek to postpone death, anyone has the right to fasten the noose as though from kindness and with a rebuke to deprive him of his life. It is likewise their custom to remove from life those who have been crippled or are suffering from incurable diseases. For they consider the greatest of evils to be for a person to desire to live when unable to do anything that makes life worth living. Wherefore, one can see that all Trogodytes are sound of body and still in the prime of life since none is over sixty years of age.

7.

The Ostrich Eaters

The Trogodytes were not the only non-civilized populations encountered by Ptolemaic explorers in Nubia. In the steppes east of Meroë lived various small populations whose lives were based on the hunting of wild animals. The most detailed of the extant descriptions of such peoples is that concerning the "Ostrich Eaters."

Towards the west of these hunters, whom the nomads are accustomed to call "Unclean," lives a branch of the Aithiopians, whom people call Simi[47] and to the south a people that is not large, those called Ostrich Eaters.[48] For, there is found in their territory a species of bird whose nature is mixed with that of a land animal whence it has received a composite name. In size it is not inferior to the largest deer. It has been formed by nature with a long neck, rounded flanks and feathers. It has a small weak head, but it possesses strong thighs and legs with cloven feet. it is unable to fly because of its weight, but it is the fastest runner of all animals, barely touching the ground with the tips of its toes. Especially when the winds blow it raises its wings and is borne along like a ship running under sail. It defends itself against pursuers by unexpectedly hurling hand-sized stones backwards with its feet. But when it is chased in calm weather, since its wings quickly collapse, it is unable to make use of its natural advantages and is easily overtaken and

51

captured.

These creatures exist in unspeakable abundance in the area, and the barbarians devise all kinds of stratagems for hunting them. Some hunt these birds with bows and arrows. Others, having dressed themselves in the skins of ostriches, conceal their right arm in the neck portion and move it just as the animals move their necks, while with their left hand they scatter seeds from a pouch hanging by their side. Luring the birds in this way, they herd them into ravines. Here men, who are standing in wait, strike them down with clubs.

They eat their meat and use their skins for clothing and bedding. When these people are attacked by the Aithiopians called Simi, they defend themselves against their attackers by using the horns of gazelles as defensive weapons. These horns, which are long and sharp, are very useful and common in the area because of the abundance of the animals that possess them.

II

KUSH AND ROME

8.

First Contact between Rome and Kush: The Triumphal Inscription of Cornelius Gallus

Relations between Ptolemaic Egypt and Kush declined sharply following the cessation of organized elephant hunting at the end of the third century B.C.E. An important consequence of that decline was that the flow of new ethnographic information concerning Nubia into Egypt virtually ceased for almost two centuries. Only with the Roman conquest of Egypt in 30 B.C.E. were permanent relations with Kush restored. The first tangible evidence of that restored contact is the triumphal inscription set up on the island of Philae by Cornelius Gallus, the first Prefect of Egypt, in which Gallus claims to have forced the king of Kush to accept the suzerainty of Rome.

Gaius Cornelius Gallus,[1] son of Gnaeus, a Roman equestrian, first Prefect of Alexandria and Egypt[2] after the kings had been conquered by Caesar, the son of the god,[3] victor over the revolt of the Thebaid[4] in 15 days, during which he defeated the enemy twice in battle, and conqueror of 5 cities: Boresis, Coptus, Ceramice, Thebes, Ophieon. After he captured the leaders of the revolts, he led his army beyond the Nile cataract into a region into which arms had not been brought before either by the Roman people or by the kings of Egypt.[5] When

the Thebaid, the common terror of all kings,[6] had been subdued, he received ambassadors of the king of the Aithiopians
and accepted that king into (Roman) protection. He also
appointed a local governor for the district of Aithiopia (known
as the) Triacontaschoenus.[7] He made this dedication[8] to the
ancestral gods and to his helper the Nile.

9.

Peace between Rome and Kush
(20 B.C.E.)

Cornelius Gallus' confidence in Meroitic acceptance of Roman suzerainty was premature. At the first sign of the relaxation of Roman vigilance, the Kushites revolted, occupied the whole of Lower Nubia, and sacked the important frontier town of Syene, modern Aswan. It required two raids deep into the Sudan conducted by the Prefect of Egypt, C. Petronius, in 24 and 22 B.C.E. to restore a semblance of order to the southern frontier of Roman Egypt. The account of the Greek geographer Strabo, a personal friend of Petronius, highlights the military achievements of his friend and the weakness of the Kushites. However, the concessions made by Augustus to the ambassadors of the Candace in the negotiations at Samos combined with the discovery at Meroë of a splendid bronze head of Augustus—surely one of those looted from Syene—and representations of Roman prisoners indicate that Petronius' victories were less decisive than Strabo's account suggests. In fact, the Romans withdrew from all of Nubia except for a seventy-mile stretch of the Nile Valley south of the First Cataract, the so-called Dodecaschoenus, as a result of the Treaty of Samos, leaving Kush free of foreign domination for over three centuries until it was finally conquered in the fourth century C.E. by the kingdom of Axum.

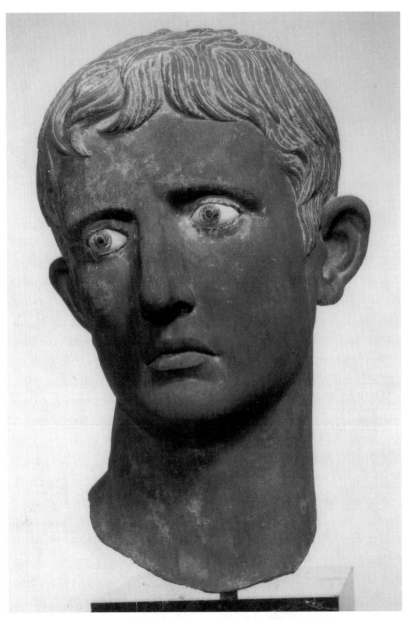

Bronze Head of Augustus. Meroë. Ca. 25 B.C.E.
Photograph courtesy of the British Museum.

Egypt was from the first disposed to peace, because the country was self-sufficient and because it was difficult of access to strangers. It was protected on the north by a harborless coast and the Egyptian Sea; on the east and west by the desert mountains of Libya and Arabia . . . . The remaining parts towards the south are occupied by the Aithiopians who live above Syene: the Trogodytes, Blemmyes, Nubae, and Megabari.[9] These peoples are nomads, and they are neither numerous nor warlike. They were, however, thought so by the ancients, because they frequently attacked defenseless persons like robbers. The Aithiopians, who extend towards the south and Meroë, are also neither numerous nor united. For they inhabit a long, narrow, and winding tract of land on the riverside. . . ; nor are they well prepared either for war or the pursuit of any other mode of life.

At present the whole country is in the same pacific state. Proof of this fact is that the Romans employ three cohorts and these are not complete to guard the upper country. Whenever the Aithiopians have ventured to attack them, it has been at the risk of danger to their own country. The rest of the forces in Egypt are neither very numerous, nor did the Romans ever once employ them collected into one army. For neither are the Egyptians themselves of a warlike disposition, nor the surrounding nations, although their numbers are very large.

Cornelius Gallus,[10] the first governor of the country appointed by (Augustus) Caesar, attacked the city of Heroönpolis, which had revolted, and took it with a small body of men. He suppressed also in a short time an insurrection in the Thebaïd, which originated because of the tribute. Later Petronius[11] resisted with his personal guard a mob of thousands of Alexandrians, who attacked him by throwing stones. He killed some and compelled the rest to desist. . . .

The Aithiopians, emboldened because a part of the forces in Egypt were drawn off by Aelius Gallus for the war against the Arabs,[12] invaded the Thebaïd, and attacked the garrison, consisting of three cohorts, near Syene. They surprised and took Syene, Elephantine, and Philae, by a sudden assault; enslaved the inhabitants, and threw down the statues of Caesar. But Petronius, marching with less than 10,000 infantry and 800 horse against an enemy of 30,000 men, first compelled them to retreat to Pselchis, an Aithiopian city.[13] He then sent deputies to demand the return of what they had taken, and to ask why they had begun the war. On their replying that they had been ill-treated by the *nomarchs*,[14] he answered, that these were not the rulers of the country but Caesar. When they asked for three days for consideration, and did nothing which they should have done, Petronius attacked and compelled them to fight. They quickly fled, being badly commanded and poorly armed. For they carried large shields made of raw hides, and axes for offensive weapons. Some, however, had pikes, and others swords. Some of them were driven into the city, others fled into the uninhabited country. Some crossed the river and escaped to a neighboring island, because there were not many crocodiles there because of the current.

Among the fugitives, were the generals of Candace, the queen of the Aithiopians in our time. She was a masculine woman, who had lost an eye. Petronius pursued them in rafts and ships, captured them all, and despatched them immediately to Alexandria. He then attacked Pselchis and took it. If we add the number of those who fell in battle to the number of prisoners, very few could have escaped.

From Pselchis Petronius went to Premnis,[15] a strong city, traveling over the hills of sand, where the army of Cambyses was overwhelmed by a sand storm.[16] He took the fortress at the first assault, and afterwards advanced to Napata. This was the royal residence of Candace;[17] and her son was there. She herself, however, was in a neighboring stronghold. When she sent ambassadors to discuss peace, and to offer the return of the prisoners brought from Syene, and the statues,[18] Petronius attacked and took Napata, from which her son had fled, and then razed it. He made prisoners of the inhabitants, and returned back again with the booty, as he judged any further advance into the country would be difficult. He strengthened, however, the fortifications of Premnis. After leaving a garrison there with two years' provisions for four hundred men, he returned to Alexandria. Some of the prisoners were publicly sold as booty, and a thousand were sent to Caesar, who had lately returned from Cantabria.[19] Others died of various diseases.

In the meantime Candace attacked the garrison with an army of many thousands of men. Petronius came to its assistance; and, entering the fortress before the enemy arrived, secured the place by many expedients. The enemy sent ambassadors, but he ordered them to go to Caesar. On their replying that they did not know who Caesar was, nor where they were to find him, Petronius appointed persons to conduct them to his presence. They arrived at Samos, where Caesar was at that time, and from whence he was on the point of proceeding into Syria, having already despatched Tiberius into Armenia. The ambassadors obtained all that they desired, and Caesar even remitted the tribute which he had imposed.[20]

10.

Kush in the First Century C.E.: Nero's Aithiopian Expedition

The first two centuries C.E. can with justification be called the "Golden Age" of Meroë. Population grew and new settlements were founded throughout Kushite territory, numerous new temples were built at Meroë city and other sites in the Island of Meroë, and trade flourished between Kush and Roman Egypt. Archaeological evidence indicates that the high point of this renaissance of Kushite culture occurred about the mid-first century C.E. during the joint reign of Queen Natakamani and King Amanitore. Surprisingly, however, a military reconnaissance party sent to explore Upper Nubia by the Roman Emperor Nero in 61 C.E. reported that Meroë was an impoverished and unimpressive city. Two considerations probably account for this conflict between the ancient written sources and the results of modern archaeology.

First, the African character of Meroitic architecture with its reliance on mud-brick and perishable materials did not impress Roman officers whose ideas of a city were based on the massive stone architecture typical of Rome and other Mediterranean cities. Second, although their own reports indicated that Meroitic influence covered much of the central and southern Sudan, the realities of contemporary Kush did not match the exaggerated expectations of Greek and

Roman writers such as Pliny, whose ideas about the extent of "Aithiopia" were based on historicized versions of Greek myths such as those of Perseus and Andromeda and Memnon. Nevertheless, Pliny's discussion of Nero's expedition and its results remains the most valuable source for the history of contact between Meroë and Rome in the Hellenistic and early Roman periods.

These are the names of places given as far as Meroë; but at the present day hardly any of them on either side of the Nile are in existence.[21] At all events, the praetorian troops[22] that were sent by the Emperor Nero under the command of a tribune, for the purposes of inquiry, when, among his other wars, he was contemplating an expedition against Aithiopia, brought back word that they had met with nothing but deserts on their route. Roman arms also penetrated into these regions in the time of the Emperor Augustus under the command of P. Petronius, a man of Equestrian rank and prefect of Egypt.[23] That general captured some of the cities there. We will mention only the ones we have found: Pselcis, Primis, Abuncis, Phthuris, Cambusis, Attenia, and Stadissis, where the river Nile, as it thunders through the cataract, has deafened the people living there.[24] He also sacked the town of Napata. The furthest distance beyond Syene to which he penetrated was nine hundred and seventy miles. Nevertheless, it was not Roman arms that rendered these regions a desert. Aithiopia was gradually worn down by wars with Egypt in which it was alternately victorious and defeated, although it had been a famous and powerful state until the Trojan War when Memnon was its king. It is also clear from the stories about Andromeda that it ruled Syria and the shores of the Mediterranean in the time of king Cepheus.[25]

Similarly, there have also been conflicting accounts concerning the extent of this country, first by Dalion who traveled a considerable distance by Meroë, and after him by Aristocreon and Basilis, as well as Simonides the Younger, who stayed at Meroë for five years, while he wrote his account of Aithiopia. Timosthenes, however, the commander of the fleets of Ptolemy Philadelphus, although he gives no other estimate as to the distance, says that Meroë is sixty days' journey from Syene.[26] Eratosthenes states that the distance is six hundred and twenty-five miles, and Artemidorus six hundred. Sebosus says that from the northernmost point of Egypt the distance to Meroë is sixteen hundred and seventy-five miles, while the other writers mentioned above make it twelve hundred and fifty.[27] This whole dispute, however, has now been settled, since the explorers sent by Nero[28] have reported that the distance from Syene to Meroë is eight hundred and seventy-one miles. The following are the stages: from Syene to Hiera Sycaminos fifty-four miles, from there to Tama seventy-two miles through the country of the Aithiopian Eunomites, one hundred and twenty, to Primis one hundred and twenty miles, to Pitara twenty-five miles, and to Tergedus one hundred and six miles.

They also state that the island of Gagaudes is half-way between Syene and Meroë, and that it is at this place that the birds called parrots were first seen, and that after another island named Articula they first saw the *sphinx*[29] monkey and after Tergedus baboons. The distance from there to Napata is eighty miles, that little town being the only one of all of them that now survives. From there to the island of Meroë, the distance is three hundred and sixty miles.

They also state that the grass near Meroë begins to be greener and there is some woodland, as well as traces of rhinoceroses and elephants. They reported also that the city of Meroë is located at a distance of seventy miles from the entrance to the island of Meroë. Opposite it as one goes up the river on the right is another island which forms a harbor. The buildings in the city, they said, were few in number. They also said that a woman named Candace ruled it, a name that has been passed on from queen to queen for many years.[30] There is a temple of Hammon[31] there, which is particularly revered. There are also shrines of Hammon throughout the whole country.

In addition, they say that when the Aithiopians ruled their empire, the island of Meroë was very famous, and that, according to tradition, it used to maintain two hundred thousand soldiers, and four thousand craftsmen. At the present day there are said to be forty-five other Aithiopian kings.[32]

11.

A Roman Soldier and his God in Nubia: The Mandulis Hymn of Paccius Maximus

The bleak description of conditions in Nubia brought back by Nero's explorers discouraged any thought of possible Roman military activity in Upper Nubia. Until the final Roman withdrawal from Nubia in 297 C.E., the border between Kush and Roman Egypt remained where Augustus had drawn it in 20 B.C.E. at the southern end of the Dodecaschoenus. The Roman soldiers who guarded this remote frontier of the Empire lived in a region in which the cultures of Kush, Egypt, and the Graeco-Roman Mediterranean met. A unique insight into their reaction to this cultural mixture is provided by the following hymn to a local Sun god, Mandulis, composed by a Roman soldier named Paccius Maximus in the late first or early first century C.E. What is particularly striking about this remarkable poem is how Paccius Maximus, although himself apparently of Nubian descent, uses the language and imagery of Greek myth to describe his deity.

(1–28) When[33] I had come to gaze on this blessed place of peace,[34] And to let wander free in the air the inspiration desired by my soul, a way of life strange to me stirred my mind from all sides. As I could not convict myself of any evil, my nature then urged me to cultivate mystic toil.

In my wisdom I then composed a complex song, having received from the gods a holy and expressive idea. When it was clear that the Muse had accomplished something pleasing to the gods, I shook out my festival song, like the flower of a green shoot on Helicon. Then a cave enticed me to enter and sleep, although I was a little afraid to yield to a dream of fantasy. Sleep picked me up and swiftly bore me away to a dear land. I seemed to be gently washing my body in the flowing streams of a river with the bountiful waters of the sweet Nile. I imagined that Calliope, a holy member of the Muses, sang together with all the nymphs a sacred song.

Thinking there still remained a bit of Greece, I set down in written form the idea which my wise soul had inspired in me. Just as one moving his body in time to music beaten by a staff, I summoned rhythm as a partner for the inscription of my song, leaving those of a critical bent little reason for blame. The leader urged me to speak my clever poem.

Then great Mandulis, glorious, came down from Olympus. He charmed away the barbaric speech of the Aithiopians[35] and urged me to sing in sweet Greek verse. He came with brilliant cheeks on the right hand of Isis, exulting in his greatness and the glory of the Romans, and uttering Pythian oracles like an Olympian god.

(29–32) You declared how because of you men can look forward to a livelihood, how day and night and all the seasons revere you and call you Breith[36] and Mandulis, fraternal gods, stars who rise as a sign of the gods in heaven.

(33–36) And you yourself told me to inscribe these clever verses, in order that they be viewed by all without flattery.

[————————————————————————]

[. . . .] trusting in the first twenty-two (*sic*) letters.[37]

12.

Isis of Philae: Mistress of Nubia: The Graffito of Pasan, son of Paese (April 10, 253 C.E.)

Our inability to read Meroitic means that the Meroitic perspective rarely appears in the sources. An exception is provided by an important group of Demotic graffiti from Philae that were written on the walls of the great temple of Isis by Meroitic pilgrims and ambassadors to memorialize their devotion to the goddess. The most extensive and revealing of these texts is that of Pasan, son of Paese. Pasan held the office of Great Envoy of Rome (the representative of the King of Meroë to the Prefect of Egypt) in the mid-third century C.E. In the third century C.E., Meroitic involvement in the affairs of the Dodecaschoenus increased. Pasan's graffitto, despite its occasional obscurity, provides important evidence not only about his personal devotion to Isis but also about relations between the Temple of Isis at Philae and the Meroitic government of Lower Nubia.

The prayer of Pasan, son of Paese, his mother being...., the *qeren-akrere* of the king,[38] the great envoy of Rome, here before Isis of Philae and the Abaton,[39] the great goddess, the good relief of this year that brings wealth, the mistress of the south, the north, the east, and the west, hearer of petitions of them that are far off.

I came to Egypt and fulfilled the orders which my master had commanded me. I performed them. He also commanded me to weigh out ten talents of silver[40] and to bring them to the temple of Isis for the prophets and the priests and the female priestly children. I caused them to be weighed out in the name of the king[41] our lord among(?) their sweetmeats . . . He commanded me to cause the entire nome[42] to celebrate, and we did it in his good name, and made a fine festival for the nome. He also commanded the king's son[43] and the *qerens* of Isis to come to Egypt with me (and remain) until we performed the festivals and the banquets which were held in the temple of Isis and the entire city.

Year 2,[44] I came to Egypt, having sung a song of triumph upon this desert through the work of Isis, the great goddess, for allowing it, for she heard our prayers and brought us safe to Egypt.

Year 3 Choiak, day 1,[45] we came to Philae. The *qerens* of Isis were with me. The prophets and the priests and the people of the city offered fine honors to me until we were taken to the temple of Isis. We made offerings in return for the life-breath of the king Teqriramane,[46] my Master. We also presented the ten talents which Teqriramane the king our Master had commanded to be brought to the temple of Isis. I brought them and offered them all together. Moreover, in spite of my being poor, in the name of the king my Master, I gave my tithe. I also fulfilled my commission and made an offering with the gold pieces which my master had given to me (to offer) before his mother Isis. We added another gold piece to them and made them into a ewer of gold and engraved it with the name of our Master. The above-mentioned gold pieces amounted to $4^1/2$ pounds. Wayankiye, the general of the river,[47] sent two pounds of gold, and they were fashioned into a golden sistrum to carry before Isis on the three decads.[48] Moreover, Pasan and Qeren, his brother, sent one pound of gold, and we made it into a ritual vase for libation to Osiris Onuris[49] the great god.

From Choiak day 1 to Pharmuthi day 1,[50] we made festival in the temple of Isis with our brethren, the *qerens* of Isis and the prophets together with the seers of the priests of Isis. We spent eight days feasting on the entry-way[51] of (the temple of) Isis on wine, beer and flesh. The people of the whole city made merry, presenting the prayer of the king, their sovereign.[52] In spite of our poverty, we also made our own banquets in the name of the king our master. I also gave 2 pounds of gold for a drinking cup with a bust of Isis within it.

Pharmuthi day 1, Abratoye, the king's son,[53] came to Philae, and we made a festival with him in the temple of Isis. He brought a ritual vase also of gold which Teqriramane sent to the temple of Isis, amounting to 3 1/2 pounds, with other three pounds which he made into a censer of gold. My mistress Isis, you who apportion lands to the gods, hearken unto me that I may be taken to Meroë, the beautiful city of your beloved soil, and keep me safe on that high desert, together with the things for which I came, to take them to your beloved son, the king Teqriramane; and bring me to Egypt with my brother(?) Harwoj, the *qeren-akrere*, the great ambassador of Rome, my good colleague; and the front of the door(?) of the king, and bring it to us to Egypt [together with the king's gifts(?); and] give to us the glorious(?) path to take them to Caesar that we may bring the prophetship of Isis to your beautiful throne.

My mistress, you who apportion lands, Isis, you are the grain-goddess(?) of the road . . . . ; our hearts depend upon you on the way, to bring us to the path of life; and we cry unto you at all times saying "hearken unto us." I am your good servant, Isis; there is no path [without you(?)] .... my heart depends upon you in Egypt, in Meroë, and in the deserts.

O Isis, this only brother that I have, I am about to leave him, and I say to you "keep him safe until you bring me to Egypt again(?), [and conduct us safe to Meroë the beautiful city of your beloved son] Teqriramane, the king, our Master."

O Isis, the prayers which I have made to you in the wilderness(?) when I strayed and cried to you and you heard me, saying ["you(?) shall] hearken to me [though I be far away(?)" and you brought me] safe. And the tributes which the king my master gave to me saying "Take them before Isis." I did bring them.

He that shall erase this prayer his name shall be cut off . . .[54]

Written in year 3 of Autocrator Caesar Gaius Vibius Trebonianus Gallus and his son,[55] the august kings, Pharmuthi day 15,[56] this happy day.

13.

The Roman Withdrawal
from Nubia (298 C.E.)

The Roman occupation of Lower Nubia ended in 298 C.E., when the Emperor Diocletian evacuated all Roman troops from the Dodecaschoenus. The only source for this important event is provided by the sixth century C.E. historian Procopius, whose account, unfortunately, is marred by several errors. The most serious of these errors is his anachronistic placement of the Nobatai in Lower Nubia in the third century C.E., when contemporary sources indicate that the principal beneficiaries of Diocletian's actions were the Blemmyes. Of particular interest in Procopius' account is the information he provides about the religion of the Blemmyes and the important role that diplomatic considerations concerning security in Lower Nubia played in ensuring the survival of traditional Egyptian religious practices at Philae, long after the conversion of most of the rest of Roman Egypt to Christianity in the fourth and fifth centuries C.E.

From the city of Auxomis[57] to the Egyptian border of the Roman Empire, where the city known as Elephantine is situated, is a journey of thirty days for a man who travels light.[58] Among the many peoples settled there are the Blemmyes and the Nobatai, very populous tribes. But the Blemmyes[59] inhabit the interior of this country, while the Nobatai[60] possess the lands on either side of the River Nile.

Formerly, however, these were not the limits of the Roman Empire, which extend approximately another seven days' journey further beyond.[61] But when the Roman Emperor Diocletian (284–305 C.E.) came there, he perceived that the tribute from those places was of the least possible account, for the following reasons: The (arable) land there is extremely narrow, since not far from the Nile exceedingly lofty cliffs rise up and fill the rest of the country. In addition, a very large number of troops had been stationed there from of old, and the Treasury was excessively burdened by the expenses for these. At the same time the Nobatai, formerly settled around the city Oasis,[62] were forever ravaging and plundering all the places there. For all these reasons, Diocletian persuaded those barbarians to migrate from their own haunts and to settle on either side of the Nile, promising to present them with great cities and with a large territory markedly better than that which they formerly inhabited. In this way he supposed they would stop harassing the territories around Oasis and also, taking possession of the land which was given to them, probably drive off the Blemmyes and the other barbarians, since the land was (now) their own. This pleased the Nobatai, and they made the migration very quickly indeed in the way Diocletian commanded them.[63] So they took possession of both the Roman cities and all the country on both sides of the river beyond the city of Elephantine.

Then this emperor decreed that there be given to them and to the Blemmyes each a stated amount of gold on the condition that they no longer plunder Roman territory.[64] Although they have been receiving this right down to my day, none the less they continue to overrun the places in those parts. Thus, it seems, with regard to all barbarians, it is simply not possible for them to keep faith with the Romans unless through fear of active defense forces.

Even so this emperor chose an island in the river Nile somewhere very near the city of Elephantine and constructed there a really strong fortification, and in that place he founded some temples and altars for the Romans and for these very barbarians in common and settled in this fortification priests of both peoples, in the expectation that their friendship would be secure for the Romans because of their participation in the rites. This is the reason why he named the place Philae.[65] Both these peoples, the Blemmyes and the Nobatai, revere all the other gods in which pagans believe, as well as Isis and Osiris, and not least Priapus. But the Blemmyes even have the custom of sacrificing human beings to the Sun. These barbarians retained the sanctuaries in Philae right down to my day,[66] but the Emperor Justinian (527–565 C.E.) decided to pull them down. Accordingly Narses, a Persarmenian by birth, whom I mentioned before as having deserted to the Romans, and who was in command of the troops there, pulled down the sanctuaries on the emperor's orders, held the priests under guard, and sent the images to Byzantium.[67]

III

THE RISE OF AXUM AND THE DECLINE OF KUSH

14.

Red Sea Trade and the Emergence of the Kingdom of Axum

Although South Arabian settlement in Ethiopia and Eritrea may have begun as early as the mid-first millennium B.C.E., the first mention of Axum occurs in the Periplus of the Erythraean Sea. *Written by an anonymous sea captain from Roman Egypt most probably in the 70s C.E., the* Periplus of Erythraean Sea *is a practical guide to conditions encountered by merchants sailing to East Africa and India. The* Periplus *reveals that already in the first century C.E. much of the trade between northeast Africa and the Red Sea passed through Axum and its port Adulis, and that Greek influence had begun to have a significant impact on the culture of the kingdom.*

Of the designated ports on the Erythraean Sea (Red Sea),[1] and the market-towns around it, the first is the Egyptian port of Mussel Harbor (Myos Hormos).[2] To those sailing down from that place, on the right hand, after eighteen hundred stadia,[3] there is Berenice. The harbors of both are at the boundary of Egypt, and are bays opening from the Erythraean Sea.

On the right-hand coast next below Berenice is the country of the Barbarians. Along the shore are the Fish-Eaters,[4] living in scattered caves in the narrow valleys. Further inland are the Barbarians, and beyond them the Wild-Flesh-Eaters and Calf-

Eaters, each tribe governed by its chief; and behind them, further inland, in the country toward the west, there lies a city called Meroë .

Below the Calf-Eaters there is a little market-town on the shore after sailing about four thousand stadia from Berenice, called Ptolemais of the Hunts, from which the hunters started for the interior under the dynasty of the Ptolemies.[5] This market-town has the true land-tortoise in small quantity; it is white and the shell is rather small. And here also is found a little ivory, like that of Adulis. But the place has no harbor and is reached only by small boats.

Below Ptolemais of the Hunts, at a distance of about three thousand stadia, there is Adulis,[6] a port established by law, lying at the inner end of a bay that runs in toward the south. Below the harbor lies the so-called Mountain Island, about two hundred stadia sea-ward from the very head of the bay, with the shores of the mainland close to it on both sides. Ships bound for this port now anchor here because of attacks from the land. They used formerly to anchor at the very head of the bay, by an island called Diodorus, close to the shore, which could be reached on foot from the land; by which means the barbarous natives attacked the island. Opposite Mountain Island, on the mainland twenty stadia[7] from shore, lies Adulis, a fair-sized village, from which there is a three-days journey to Coloe, an inland town and the first market for ivory. From that place to the city of the people called Axumites there is a five days' journey more; to that place all the ivory is brought from the country beyond the Nile through the district called Cyeneum,[8] and thence to Adulis. Practically the whole number of elephants and rhinoceroses that are killed live in the places inland, although at rare intervals they are hunted on the seacoast even near Adulis.[9] Before the harbor of that market-town, out at sea on the right hand, there lie a great many little sandy islands called Alalaei,[10] yielding tortoise-shell, which is brought to market there by the Fish-Eaters.

And about eight hundred stadia beyond there is another very deep bay, with a great mound of sand piled up at the right of the entrance; at the bottom of which obsidian is found, and this is the only place where it is produced. These places, from the Calf-Eaters to the other Barbarian country, are governed by Zoscales;[11] who is miserly in his ways and always striving for more, but otherwise upright, and acquainted with Greek literature.

There are imported into these places, undressed cloth made in Egypt for the Barbarians; robes from Arsinoe; cloaks of poor quality dyed in colors; double-fringed linen mantles; many kinds of glass stones and others of millefiori glass made in Thebes; and brass, which is used for ornament and in cut pieces instead of coin; sheets of soft copper, used for cooking-utensils and cut up for bracelets and anklets for the women; iron, which is made into spears used against the elephants and other wild beasts, and in their wars. Besides these, small axes are imported, and adzes and swords; copper drinking-cups, round and large; a little Roman money for resident foreigners; wine of Laodicea and Italy, not much; olive oil, not much; for the king, gold and silver plate made after the fashion of the country, and for clothing, military cloaks and thin coats of skin, of no great value. Likewise from the district of Ariaca across this sea, there are imported Indian iron, and steel, and Indian cotton cloth; the broad cloth called *monaché* and that called *sag-matogêné*,[12] and girdles, and coats of skin and mallow-colored cloth, and a few muslins, and colored lac. There are exported from these places ivory, and tortoise-shell and rhinoceros-horn.[13] The most from Egypt is brought to this market from the month of January to September, that is, from Tybi to Thoth; but seasonably they put to sea about the month of September.

15.

The Empire of Axum

The survival of ancient texts often depends on fortunate accidents. The text translated below is a striking example of such an accident. The original inscription is lost. Its text survives, however, because an Axumite governor of the port of Adulis in the sixth century C.E. asked a visiting Greek merchant named Cosmas Indicopleustes ("The India-Sailor") to copy it. Cosmas later included his copy of the inscription in a book he wrote entitled The Christian Topography. *The inscription celebrates the creation by a pagan Axumite king in the second or third century C.E. of an empire centered at Axum that included most of modern Ethiopia and Yemen. Particularly noteworthy is the king's reference to the creation of a road that would enable merchants to travel directly from Axum to Egypt, thereby helping impoverish Kush by diverting commerce from the Nile route.*

Having[14] after this with a strong hand compelled the nations bordering on my kingdom to live in peace, I made war upon the following nations, and by force of arms reduced them to subjection. I warred first with the nation of Gaze,[15] then with Agame and Sigye, and having conquered them I exacted the half of all that they possessed. I next reduced Aua and Tiamo, called Tziamo, and the Gambela, and the tribes near them, and Zingabene and Angabe and Tiama and Athagaus and Kalaa, and the Semenoi—a people who lived beyond the Nile on

Triumphal throne bases. Axum.
Photograph courtesy of Professor David W. Phillipson.

mountains difficult of access and covered with snow, where the year is all winter with hailstorms, frosts and snows into which a man sinks knee-deep. I next subdued Lazine and Zaa and Gabala, tribes which inhabit mountains with steep declivities abounding with hot springs, the Atalmo and Bega,[16] and all the tribes in the same quarter along with them

I proceeded next against the Tangaïtae, who adjoin the borders of Egypt; and having reduced them I made a footpath giving access by land into Egypt from that part of my dominions. Next I reduced Annine and Metine—tribes inhabiting precipitous mountains. My arms were next directed against the Sesea nation. These had retired to a high mountain difficult of access; but I blockaded the mountain on every side, and compelled them to come down and surrender. I then selected for myself the best of their young men and their women, with their sons and daughters and all besides that they possessed. The tribes of Rhausi I next brought to submission: a barbarous race spread over wide waterless plains in the interior of the frankincense country. [Advancing thence towards the sea] I encountered the Solate, whom I subdued, and left with instructions to guard the coast.

All these nations, protected though they were by mountains that were all but impregnable, I conquered, after engagements in which I was myself present. Upon their submission I restored their territories to them, subject to the payment of tribute. Many other tribes besides these submitted of their own accord, and became likewise tributary. And I sent a fleet and land forces against the Arabitae and Cinaedocolpitae who dwelt on the other side of the Red Sea, and having reduced the sovereigns of both, I imposed on them a land tribute and charged them to make traveling safe both by sea and land. I thus subdued the whole coast from Leuke Kome to the country of the Sabaeans.[17]

I first and alone of the kings of my race made these conquests. For this success I now offer my thanks to my mighty God, Ares, who begat me, and by whose aid I reduced all the nations bordering on my country, on the East to the country of frankincense, and on the West to Aithiopia and Sasu. Of these expeditions, some were conducted by myself in person, and ended in victory, and the others I entrusted to my officers. Having thus brought all the world under my authority to peace, I came down to Adulis and offered sacrifice to Zeus, and to Ares and to Poseidon,[18] whom I entreated to befriend all who go down to the sea in ships. Here also I reunited all my forces, and setting down this Chair[19] in this place, I consecrated it to Ares in the twenty-seventh year of my reign.

16.

Ezana and the Bega

Prosperity and security for the kingdoms of Kush and Axum depended in large part on their ability to control the pastoral nomads who lived in the deserts between the Nile and Red Sea. In this inscription composed prior to his conversion to Christianity, the fourth century C.E. Axumite king Ezana tells how he suppressed a rebellion by the most important of these nomadic peoples, the Bega.

Ezana,[20] King of Axum and of Himyar, and of Raidan, and of Aithiopia, and of Saba, and of Salhen, and of Siyanio, and of Bega, and of Kasu, the King of Kings, the son of the invincible god Ares.[21] As the peoples of the Bega had rebelled,[22] we sent our brothers Shai'azana and Hadefan to make war on them. And having laid down their arms, our brothers subdued them and brought them to us with their camp-followers, and 3,112 cattle and 6,224 sheep and pack animals, giving them sufficient cattle and grain to eat, and beer and wine and water to drink according to their number. They received each day 22,000 wheaten cakes and wine for four months, while they were bringing them to us. These we allowed, having provided them with all kinds of food and given them clothes, to depart, and they settled in a district belonging to our realm, which is called Matlia.[23] And we commanded again that food should be given to them, and we granted to the six kinglets[24] 25,140 cattle. To obtain the favor of my begetter, the invincible Ares, I have set up to him one statue in gold and one in silver, and three in copper, for good.

17.

Protection of Axumite Trade

Commerce provided much of the wealth of the kingdom of Axum, and from its earliest days the kings of Axum actively fostered the caravan trade with Egypt and the interior of Africa. In this Ge'ez inscription Ezana records the punishment of a tribe that had raided and destroyed such a caravan.

Ezana, the son of Ella Amida, of the family of Halen, King of Axum, and of Himyar, and of Raydan, and of Saba, and of Salhen, and of Siamo, and of Bega, and of Kasu, the son of Mahrem, who cannot be conquered by the enemy.[25] He made war on the Sarane, whose kingdom is Afan,[26] after they had fought against us and killed a merchant caravan.

And then we made war upon them, first of all we sent armies, the army of Mahaza, and the army of Dakuen, and the army of Hara, and then we ourselves followed, and we encamped at the place where the troops were assembled in Alaha, and we made our soldiers set out from there. And they killed, and made prisoners and despoiled them. And we attacked Sa'ne and Sawante, and Gema, and Zahtan, four peoples, and we took prisoner Alita with his two children. And a slaughter took place, of the men of Afan 503, and women 202, in all 705. Of his camp-followers there were taken prisoners, men 40, and women and children 165, in all 205.[27] As spoil were carried off 31,900 and 57 cattle, baggage animals, 827.

And [the king] returned in safety together with his people. And he set up a throne here in Shado, and committed himself to the protection of Astar, and Beher, and Meder.[28] If there be anyone who would overthrow him and remove him, that person, and his land, and his family, shall be overthrown and removed, and he shall be rooted out of his country. And the king offered as a thank-offering to Mahrem, who had begotten him, 100 cattle and 50 prisoners.[29]

18.

The Axumite Gold Trade

Cosmas' goal in his The Christian Topography *was to prove that the universe was shaped like the Ark of the Covenant. To help prove his case, Cosmas included in his work much valuable geographical information that he had collected during his career as a merchant sailing between Egypt and the countries of the Red Sea basin. In this passage he describes the gold trade with the peoples of Axum's African hinterland that made Axum one of the principal sources of gold for the Roman Empire in Late Antiquity.*

That country known as that of Sasu is itself near the ocean, just as the ocean is near the frankincense country,[30] in which there are many gold mines. The King of the Axumites accordingly, every other year, through the governor of Agau,[31] sends thither special agents to bargain for the gold, and these are accompanied by many other traders—upwards, say of five hundred—bound on the same errand as themselves. They take along with them to the mining district oxen, lumps of salt, and iron, and when they reach its neighborhood they make a halt at a certain spot and form an encampment, which they fence round with a great hedge of thorns. Within this they live, and having slaughtered the oxen, cut them in pieces, and lay the pieces on the top of thorns, along with the lumps of salt and the iron. Then come the natives bringing gold in nuggets like peas, called *tancharas*, and lay one or two or more of these upon what pleases them—the pieces of flesh or the salt or the iron, and then they retire to some distance off. Then the owner of the meat approaches, and if he is satisfied he takes the gold away, and upon seeing this its owner comes and takes the flesh or the salt or the iron. If, however, he is not satisfied, he leaves the gold, when the native seeing that he has not taken it, comes and either puts down more gold, or takes up what he had laid down, and goes away. Such is the mode in which business is transacted with the people of that country, because their language is different and interpreters are hardly to be found.[32]

The time they stay in that country is five days more or less, according as the natives more or less readily coming forward buy up all their wares. On the journey homeward they all agree to travel well-armed, since some of the tribes through whose country they must pass might threaten to attack them from a desire to rob them of their gold.[33] The space of six months is taken up with this trading expedition, including both the going and the returning. In going they march very slowly, chiefly because of the cattle, but in returning they quicken their pace lest on the way, they should be overtaken by winter and its rains. For the sources of the river Nile lie somewhere in these parts, and in winter, on account of the heavy rains, the numerous rivers which they generate obstruct the path of the traveler. The people there have their winter at the time we have our summer. It begins in the month Epiphi of the Egyptians and continues till Thoth,[34] and during the three months the rain falls in torrents, and makes a multitude of rivers all of which flow into the Nile.

Not all relations with the tribes of the interior were so benign as Cosmas points out in his commentary on Document 15.

For most of the slaves which are now found in the hands of

merchants who resort to these parts are taken from the tribes of which we speak. As for the Semenai, where he [the author of no. 15] says there are snows and ice, it is to that country that the King of the Axumites expatriates anyone he has sentenced to be banished.

19.

The Introduction
of Christianity to Axum

The Christianization of Axum in the mid-fourth century C.E. was a fundamental turning point in the history of Ethiopia. It strengthened the cultural ties between Axum and Christian Egypt at the expense of the bonds that had linked it to South Arabia, thereby laying the foundation for the tension between Christian Ethiopia and Islam that has persisted to this day. In this passage the late fourth century C.E. Latin Church historian Rufinus tells the story of the Christianization of Axum as recounted to him by one of the main figures in the process, Aedesius, Bishop of Tyre. Particularly worth noting is the important role played by Christian merchants from the Roman Empire in the introduction of Christianity to Axum.

One Metrodorus, a philosopher, is said to have penetrated to further India[35] in order to view places and see the world. Inspired by his example, one Meropius, a philosopher of Tyre, wished to visit India with a similar object, taking with him two small boys who were related to him and whom he was educating in humane studies. The younger of them was called Aedesius, the other Frumentius. When, having seen and taken note of what his soul fed upon, the philosopher had begun to return, the ship on which he traveled put in for water or some other necessary at a certain port. It is the custom of the barbarians of these parts that, if ever the neighboring tribes report that their treaty with the Romans is broken, all Romans found among them should be massacred. The philosopher's ship was boarded; all with himself were put to the sword.

The boys were found studying under a tree and preparing their lessons, and, preserved by the mercy of the barbarians, were taken to the king.[36] He made one of them, Aedesius, his cupbearer. Frumentius, whom he had perceived to be sagacious and prudent, he made his treasurer and secretary. Thereafter, they were held in great honor and affection by the king. The king died, leaving his wife with an infant son as heir to the bereaved kingdom. He gave the young men liberty to do what they pleased but the queen besought them with tears, since she had no more faithful subjects in the whole kingdom, to share with her the cares of governing the kingdom until her son should grow up, especially Frumentius, whose ability was equal to guiding the kingdom—for the other, though loyal and honest of heart, was simple.

While they lived there and Frumentius held the reins of government in his hands, God stirred up his heart and he began to search out with care those of the Roman merchants[37] who were Christians and to give them great influence and to urge them to establish in various places conventicles to which they might resort for prayer in the Roman manner.[38] He himself, moreover, did the same and so encouraged the others, attracting them with his favor and his benefits, providing them with whatever was needed, supplying sites for buildings and other necessaries, and in every way promoting the growth of the seed of Christianity in the country. When the prince for whom they exercised the regency had grown up, they completed and faithfully delivered over their trust, and, though the queen and her son sought greatly to detain them and begged them to remain, returned to the Roman Empire.

Aedesius hastened to Tyre to revisit his parents and relatives. Frumentius went to Alexandria, saying that it was not right to hide the work of God. He laid the whole affair before the bishop and urged him to look for some worthy man to send as bishop over the many Christians already congregated and the churches built on barbarian soil. Then Athanasius (for he had recently assumed the episcopate),[39] having carefully weighed and considered Frumentius' words and deeds, declared in a council of the priests: "What other man shall we find in whom the Spirit of God is as in you, who can accomplish these things?" And he consecrated him and bade him return in the grace of God whence he had come. And when he had arrived in India as bishop, such grace is said to have been given to him by God that apostolic miracles were wrought by him and a countless number of barbarians were converted by him to the faith. From which time Christian peoples and churches have been created in the parts of India and the priesthood has begun. These facts I[40] know not from common report but from the mouth of Aedesius himself, who had been Frumentius' companion and was later made a priest in Tyre.

20.

The Destruction of Meroë (ca. 360 C.E.)

The steady westward expansion of Axumite territory in the second and third centuries C.E. made conflict between Axum and Kush inevitable. The reference to Ezana as King of Kasu (=Kush) in inscriptions composed before his conversion to Christianity and the discovery of fragments of two Axumite victory inscriptions at Meroë indicate that Axum had already established suzerainty over Meroë before the events recounted in this inscription. According to Ezana's account the Kushites controlled only a fragment of their former territory at the time of his campaign, the rest having been occupied by the people he refers to as the Noba. Despite the fact that Ezana's attack was directed ostensibly against the Noba, the Kushites unsuccessfully tried to block the advance of his forces when they reached the borders of Kushite territory. The resulting devastation of the remaining Kushite towns is vividly described by Ezana, and archaeologists have discovered traces of the destruction wrought by the Axumite forces at Meroë.

By[41] the power of the Lord of Heaven,[42] Who in heaven and upon earth is mightier than everything which exists, Ezana, the son of Ella Amida, a native of Halen, king of Axum and of Himyar, and of Raydan, and of Saba, and of Salhen, and of

Inscription of King Ezana. Axum. Fourth Century C.E.
Photograph courtesy of Professor David W. Phillipson.

Seyamo, and of Bega, and of Kasu, King of Kings, the son of Ella Amida, who is invincible to the enemy.

By the might of the Lord of heaven, Who has made me Lord, Who to all eternity, the Perfect One, reigns, Who is invincible to the enemy, no enemy shall stand before, and after me no enemy shall follow.

By the might of the Lord of all, I made war upon Noba, for the peoples had rebelled and had made a boast of it. And "they [the Axumites] will not cross the river Takkaze,"[43] said the peoples of Noba. And they were in the habit of attacking the peoples of Mangurto, and Khasa, and Barya, and the blacks,[44] and of making war upon the Red peoples. And twice and thrice they had broken their solemn oaths, and had killed their neighbors mercilessly, and they had stripped bare and stolen the properties of our deputies and messengers which I had sent to them to inquire into their thefts, and had stolen from them their weapons of defense. And as I had sent warnings to them and they would not hearken to me, and they refused to cease from their evil deeds, and then they betook themselves to flight, I made war upon them.

And I rose in the might of the Lord of the Land, and I fought with them on the Takkaze, at the ford of Kemalke. Thereupon they took flight, and would not make a stand. And I followed after the fugitives for twenty-three days, killing some and making prisoners others, and capturing spoil wherever I stopped. Prisoners and spoil my people who had marched into the country brought back to me. Meanwhile I burnt their towns, both those built of bricks and those built of reeds, and my soldiers carried off its food, and its copper, and its iron, and its brass, and they destroyed the statues in their houses, and the treasuries of food, and the cotton trees, and cast them into the River Seda.[45] Many people died in the water; I do not know their number. Their ships were sunk together with numerous men and women who were in them.

And I captured two nobles, who had come as spies, riding on camels.[46] Their names were Yesaka, Butale, and the chieftain Angabenawi. The following nobles were also killed: Danoke, Dagale, Anake, Haware. As for Karkara, their priest, the soldiers wounded him, and took from him a silver crown and a gold ring. Five nobles and one priest died.

And I came to Kasu[47] and I fought a battle and made prisoners of its people at the junction of the rivers Seda and Takkaze. And the day after I arrived I sent out to raid the country, the army Mahaza, and the army Hara, and Damawa, and Falha and Sera upstream of Seda, and the cities built of bricks and those of reeds. The names of the cities built of bricks were Alwa and Daro.[48] And they killed, and captured prisoners and cast people into the water . . . . And after that I sent the army of Halen, and the army of Laken . . . down the Seda against the towns of the Noba which are made of reeds—4 towns— Negus—1. The towns of brick which the Noba had taken were Tabito—1—and Fertoti—1.

And my peoples arrived at the frontier of the Red Noba[49] and they returned safe and sound, having captured prisoners and slain the Noba and taken spoil from them by the might of the Lord of Heaven. And I planted a throne in that country at the place where the Rivers Seda and Takkaze join.

IV

THE END OF ANTIQUITY

21.

The Struggle for Power in Lower Nubia: the Silko Inscription

The Roman withdrawal from the Dodecaschoenus and the subsequent destruction of Meroë by Axum set off a fierce struggle for power in Lower Nubia between the Blemmyes and the Nobatai (=Noba?). In this inscription from Kalabsha temple, which dates from the fifth century C.E., Silko, the ruler of the Nobatai, tells how he drove the Blemmyes from their Nubian strongholds and established Nobatai dominance in the region.

I Silko, Kinglet (*Basiliskos*)[1] of the Nobatai and all the Aithiopians, came to Talmis and Taphis. Twice I fought with the Blemmyes, and the god gave victory to me. On the third occasion I was victorious again and I conquered their cities. I sat down with my army for the first time. I defeated them, and they honored me. I made peace with them, and they swore by their sacred images, and I trusted their oath that they were good men. I withdrew to the upper portions of my realm.

When I became *Basiliskos*, I did not go behind the other kings (*Basileis*) at all, but before them at their head. As for those who try to contend with me, I do not allow them to occupy their lands if they do not honor me and beg me. For I am a lion in the lower lands and I am a bear[2] in the upper lands. I fought

Silko triumphant over the Blemmyes. Graffito from Kalabsha Temple (Fifth Century C.E.*). Source: Lászlo Török, Late Antique Nubia: History and archaeology of the southern neighbour of Egypt in the 4th–6th c.* A.D., *Antaeus Communicationes ex instituto Archaeologico Academiae Scientiarum Hungaricae, 16 (Budapest, 1988), Pl. 1.*

once with the Blemmyes from Primis to Talmis,[3] and I ravaged the lands of the other Nobatai in the upper countries,[4] since they tried to contend with me. The rulers of other peoples, who try to contend with me, I do not allow to sit in the shade but outside in the sun. They did not drink water in their houses. For I seize the women and children of those who are my rivals.

22.

Treaty between the Blemmyes, Nobatai, and Rome (ca. 453 C.E.)

Diocletian had ordered the withdrawal of the Roman garrisons from the Dodecaschoenus in the expectation that Meroë could impose restraint on the Blemmyes and the Nobatai. The Axumite conquest of Meroë frustrated that hope, however, leaving southern Egypt vulnerable to raids by the Blemmyes and Nobatai. The historian Priscus describes in this text how Maximinus, the military governor of the Thebaïd, negotiated a short-lived peace treaty with the Blemmyes and Nobatai in the mid-fifth century C.E.

The Blemmyes and Nobatai, having been defeated by the Romans, sent a delegation to Maximinus from both peoples, wishing to enter into a peace treaty. And they proposed that this be observed so long as Maximinus remained in the country of the Thebans. When he refused to enter into a treaty for such a short period, they said that they would not take up arms for the rest of his life. But as he would not accept even the second proposal of the embassy, they made a treaty for one hundred years. In this it was agreed that the Roman prisoners be released without ransom regardless of whether they had been captured during this or during any other attack, that the animals carried off at that time be returned, and that the compensation for their expenses be paid; further that the well born among them be handed over as hostages to guarantee the treaty, and that their crossing to the temple of Isis be unhindered in accordance with the ancient law, Egyptians having charge of the river boat in which the statue of the goddess is placed and ferried across the river. For at a stated time the barbarians bring the statue to their own country and, after having consulted it, return it safely to the island.[5]

Therefore Maximinus decided that it was appropriate that the text of the compact be ratified in the temple of Philae. Some people were sent. Also present were those of the Blemmyes and of the Nobatai who were to conclude the treaty on the island. After the terms of the agreement had been committed to writing and the hostages had been handed over—they were children of the ex-despots and former sub-despots,[6] something that had never before happened in this war, for never had children of Nobatai and of Blemmyes been hostages with the Romans—it turned out that Maximinus fell into precarious health and died. When the barbarians got word of Maximinus' death, they took away their hostages by force and overran the country.

23.

The Christianization of Nubia

The turbulent conditions in Lower Nubia described in Documents 21 and 22 did not last long. Within a century the territory of the former kingdom of Kush had been divided among three successor states: Nobatia in Lower Nubia, Makouria in the Dongola Reach, and Alwah in the area from Meroë southward. The conversion of these three kingdoms to Christianity in the mid-sixth century C.E. marked a sharp break in Nubian culture history. Almost overnight the Pharaonic forms and ideas that had dominated the culture of Kush since the second millennium B.C.E. disappeared and were replaced by artistic forms and political institutions inspired by those of the Christian Roman Empire. In this selection the sixth century C.E. church historian John of Ephesus describes the rivalry between the orthodox Roman Emperor Justinian I (527–565 C.E.) and his monophysite wife Theodora for the privilege of converting Nobatia and its southern neighbors to Christianity.

Among the clergy in attendance upon Patriarch Theodosius,[7] was a presbyter named Julian, an old man of great worth, who conceived an earnest spiritual desire to christianize the wandering people who dwell on the eastern borders of the Thebaïd beyond Egypt, and who are not only not subject to the authority of the Roman empire, but even receive a subsidy on condition that they do not enter nor pillage Egypt.[8] The blessed Julian, therefore, being full of anxiety for this people, went and spoke about them to the late queen Theodora, in the hope of awakening in her a similar desire for their conversion; and as the queen was fervent in zeal for God, she received the proposal with joy, and promised to do every thing in her power for the conversion of these tribes from the errors of idolatry. In her joy, therefore, she informed the victorious king Justinian of the proposed undertaking, and promised and anxiously desired to send the blessed Julian thither.

But when the king heard that the person she intended to send was opposed to the Council of Chalcedon,[9] he was not pleased, and determined to write to the bishops of his own side in the Thebaïd, with orders for them to proceed thither and instruct them, and plant among them the name of the synod. And as he entered upon the matter with great zeal, he sent thither, without a moment's delay, ambassadors with gold and baptismal robes, and gifts of honor for the king of that people, and letters for the duke of the Thebaïd,[10] enjoining him to take every care of the embassy, and escort them to the territories of the Nobatai.

Theodora, however, learned of Justinian's plan and wrote to the Duke of the Thebaïd, ordering him to delay the emperor's representatives in order that Julian might reach the Nobatai first.

The blessed Julian, meanwhile, and the ambassadors who accompanied him, had arrived at the confines of the Nobatai,[11] whence they sent to the king and his princes, informing him of their coming. Upon which an armed escort set out, who received them joyfully, and brought them into their land unto the king. And he too received them with pleasure, and her majesty's letter was presented, and read to him, and the purport of it explained. They accepted also the magnificent honors sent them, and the numerous baptismal robes, and every thing else richly provided for their use. And immediately with joy they yielded themselves up, and utterly abjured the error of their forefathers, and confessed the God of the Christians, saying, "that He is the one true God, and there is no other beside."

Meanwhile Justinian's emissary arrived and was granted an audience by the king of the Nobatai.

And when he had obtained an audience, he also gave the king the letters and presents, and began to inform and tell him, according to his instructions, as follows: "The king of the Romans has sent us to you, that in case of your becoming Christians, you may cleave to the church and those who govern it, and not be led astray after those who have been expelled from it." And when the king of the Nobatai and his princes heard these things, they answered them, saying, "The honorable present which the king of the Romans has sent us we accept, and will also ourselves send him a present. But his faith we will not accept. For if we consent to become Christians, we shall walk after the example of Patriarch Theodosius, who because he was not willing to accept the wicked faith of the king,[12] was driven away by him and expelled from his church. If, therefore, we abandon our heathenism and errors, we cannot consent to fall into the wicked faith professed by the king." In this manner then they sent the king's messengers away, with a written answer to the same effect.

As for the blessed Julian, he remained with them for two years, though suffering greatly from the extreme heat. For he used to say that from nine o'clock until four in the afternoon he was obliged to take refuge in caverns, full of water, where he sat undressed and girt with a linen garment, such as the people of the country wear. And if he left the water his skin, he said, was blistered by the heat. Nevertheless, he endured it patiently, and taught them, and baptized both the king and nobles, and much people also.

Eighteen years later[13] *another Nubian people, the Alodaei, who inhabited the island of Meroë and the regions to the south of it, sent two embassies to the Nobatai requesting that they arrange for a Christian missionary to be sent to them also.*

Meanwhile the king of the Alodaei[14] had...sent a second embassy to the king of the Nobatai, requesting that the bishop Longinus might be sent to teach and baptize both him and his people. And it was plainly visible that the conversion of that kingdom was the good purpose of the grace of God. The Lord therefore stirred up the spirit of Longinus to go to them; and though the Nubians were grieved at being separated from him, they nevertheless sent with him nobles and princes and men well acquainted with the desert.

Upon the journey, however, he became ill, as also did his companions. And so great were their privations, and the intensity of the heat that, as he mentions in a letter, he lost in the desert no less than seventeen camels out of the baggage animals which accompanied him. Nor was this their only or chief danger; for between the Nobatai and the Alodaei is a country inhabited by another people, called the Makoritae;[15] and when their king heard that Longinus had started on his journey, Satan in his envy stirred him up to set watchers in all the passes of his kingdom on all the roads, both in the mountains and in the plains, as far as the sea of weeds,[16] in hopes of arresting Longinus, and so hindering the salvation of the powerful people of the Alodaei. But God preserved him, and blinded the eyes of those who wanted to seize him; and he passed through them, and went on his way, and they saw him not.

And on his arrival at the borders of the kingdom to which he was traveling, the king, as he tells us in his letters, on hearing of it, sent one of his nobles to meet him, named Aitekia, who received him honorably, and made him pass over into their land with great pomp. And on approaching nearer, the king went out in person to meet him, and received him with great joy. And immediately upon his arrival, he spoke unto the king and to all his nobles the word of God, and they opened their understandings, and listened with joy to what he said; and after a few days' instruction, both the king himself was baptized and all his nobles; and, subsequently, in process of time, his people also. And so the king, being glad and joyful, wrote a letter of thanks to the king of Nobatai, as follows:

Letter of the King of Alwah to the King of the Nubians.

"Your love is remembered by us, my lord, our brother Orfiulo, because you have now shown yourself my true kinsman, and that not only in the body, but also in the spirit, in having sent to me here our common spiritual father, who has shown me the way of truth, and of the true light of Christ our God, and has baptized me and my nobles, and all my family. And in every thing the work of Christ is multiplied, and I have hope in the holy God, and am desirous moreover of doing your pleasure and driving your enemies from your land. For he is not your enemy alone, but also mine; for your land is my land, and your people my people. Let not your courage therefore fail, but be manful and take courage; for it is impossible for me to be careless of you and your land, especially now that I have become a Christian, by the help of my father, the holy father Longinus.

As we have need, however, of church furniture, get some ready for us; for I feel certain that you will send me these things with carefulness, and I will make you answer. But on the day on which I was keeping festival, I did not wish to write, lest my letters should fail. Don't be anxious, therefore, but encourage yourself, and play the man; for Christ is with us."

Such then was the letter which this new confessor, the king of the Alodaei, wrote to the king of the Nobatai. And next we will also give a short extract from a letter of the blessed Longinus, which he wrote from that land [Alwah], and sent to the king of the Nobatai, with a request that he would forward it to Alexandria; which also he did; and it is as follows:

". . . Not then to trouble you with our problems, and make the letter tedious. I have omitted all such matters, and will tell you, secondly, that which will rejoice all who are real Christians, and strict members of the orthodox communion; and I do rejoice with you all, and will rejoice, and you in like manner must rejoice with me. And, moreover, rejoice with me in this, that He Who wills that every man should be saved, and desires not the death of a sinner, such as I am, but forgets all my sins, has remembered His mercy and grace towards me, and opened for me the door of his Mercy, and delivered me from those who were hunting after my life, and led me safely through them, and blinded their eyes that they did not see me. Nor were we unvisited by his loving kindness in chastening us, in that all of us, with my unworthy self, fell ill, from the greatest even to the least; and I was the first to suffer. For it was but right that I should be chastened first, because I am guilty of many sins, and many are the offenses into which I have fallen. And not only did we become ill our selves, and despaired of our safety, but also the animals that were with us died, not being able to bear the heat, and the thirst in the mountains, and the unwholesomeness of the water, so that we lost no less than seventeen camels. And when the king of the Alodaei heard that I had determined to come to him, he sent one of his princes, named Itika, who led me with great pomp into their land.

And on our arrival at the river's bank, we went on board a vessel; and the king, hearing of our coming, rejoiced, and came out in person to meet us, received us with great joy. And by the grace of God we taught him, and have baptized him and his nobles and all his family; and the work of God grows daily. But inasmuch as there are certain Abyssinians, who have fallen into the malady of Julian, and say, that Christ suffered in a body not capable of pain, or of death,[17] we have told them what is the correct belief, and have required them to anathematize this heresy in writing, and have received these persons upon their presenting their recantation . . . . And again, after some things which we have omitted, he thus proceeds:

". . . And let all your rulers and people, on learning these things, offer up with spiritual joy their praises and thanksgivings to our merciful God, for all these His innumerable gifts; and let the fathers take care that there be sent here bishops, who will be able to labor and minister in this divine work, which is pleasing both to God and men, and in the reality of which they may feel confident, and that is going on prosperously. For there are a thousand thousand here who are hastening to salvation, to the glory of Him Who is the Savior of us all, even Christ. And believe what I say, that a short time ago a sort of purpose suggested by the weakness of human nature came to me, not to write to anyone; but when I considered the danger which those incur who are negligent in their use of spiritual gifts, I have addressed this short letter to your spiritual love. For I desire neither silver, nor gold, nor dresses, as God is my witness, Who tries the hearts of men, and Who knows all I do, and that I have not bread for my daily use, and am even glad to see with my eyes food of vegetables only. And thus far then let it suffice for me to have told you."

This then was written by the holy Longinus himself, being extracts from the letter he sent from the land of the Alodaei to the king of the Nobatai, with a request that he would forward it to Alexandria, which he accordingly did, to Theodore, whom Longinus had himself appointed as patriarch. And at the same time the king himself sent him a letter to inform him of Longinus' arrival among them and his subsequent departure, and the trials and difficulties which stood in his way, and the gracious aid which God in His goodness gave him, and so forth, writing in admiration of him, to the following effect:

Letter of the king of the Nobatai to Theodore of Alexandria.

"Before all things I especially desire your health in Christ, my blessed father; and next, my purpose is that you should know, that seven months ago the king of the powerful people of the Alodaei in Aithiopia, sent here, to obtain from me, my holy father, the bishop Longinus, to baptize him. And it was done according to all that the holy king my father wrote unto me. For when I had mentioned the matter to my father, he at once readily and with good will agreed, and in his kindness promised to visit them. And every day he urged me on, saying, We must not neglect this business, for it is of God. But because of the wicked devices of him who dwells between us, I mean the king of the Makoritae, I sent my saintly father to the king of the Blemmyes, that he might conduct him here by routes further inland. But the Makoritae heard also of this, and set people on the look out in all the passes of his kingdom, both in the mountains and in the plains, and as far as the sea of weeds, wishing to lay hands on my father, and put a stop to the good work of God, as my father has written here to tell me.

And great was the wearisomeness and the bitter trials of soul and body which he endured in the land of the Blemmyes, together with extreme privation and want. And yet even so the wicked devices of his enemy could not hinder the readiness of my saintly father in doing the work of God; and the Lord our God directed his ways and ordered his paths so that he traveled safely over long tracks of country, and escaped the strong garrisons set in his way, although he lost his retinue of camels and the other beasts of burden with him. But God helped him, and delivered him, and he arrived at the land, and was joyfully received by the king and all the people; and he taught and baptized them, as we learn from the letter which he has sent here. And this further you must know, how God the Lord of all has been with my father, and accompanied him, that you may wonder greatly at what he has done unto him. For when the king, my uncle, and his royal ancestors used to send an embassy to that kingdom [Alwah], the ambassador generally took eight or ten years in going and returning. But when my holy father went there, within two hundred days he sent an embassy to us from the king, whereas many of many of my former ambassadors had never returned here at all. And not to make my account too long, my father has sent a letter to me here which I was to forward to you; and see, I have sent them by his ambassador; and in them he has given us an account of all that has happened to him, and all that he has done. And the news which his messenger has brought us, you must make known; for it would not be right in your excellency to conceal and neglect all these matters. Rather your holiness ought to aid my saintly father by your pious prayers."

Now this portion of the letter of the king of the Nobatai we insert here in confirmation of our narrative, because he bears witness to the whole of this providential history; and he wrote two others to the same effect, which we have not been able to insert for fear of making our story too long. And inasmuch as the main purport of this divine transaction is made known to every one, and declared by means of these two letters of the bishop and the king, as we have determined not to lengthen the narrative by adding anything of our own, except to apply to these things, in token of our praise and admiration, the word of our Savior, which says, "Verily, I say unto you, that this good news of the kingdom shall be preached unto all the nations, and then shall the end be." And these things then, which are now recorded by us, were done by the help of God in the year 891.[18]

24.

Contract for the Sale of a Nubian Slave Girl (Sixth Century C.E.)

Throughout antiquity Nubia was the principal source for "Aithiopian" slaves. Because slavery was taken for granted by ancient peoples, information concerning the conduct of the slave trade is rare. The contract translated below provides a unique insight into the trade in Nubian slaves in late ancient Egypt and into the conditions under which such slaves lived.

. . . we dispose and make, we Pathermuthis, son of Khristophoros, . . . and Anatolios, son of Makarios . . . from this city of Hermupolis,[19] on the twenty-first of Thoth[20] of the current Third Indiction,[21] this written contract for Aurelia Isidora, the most well-born daughter of Viktor, from the same city of Hermupolis.

Greeting. We acknowledge that we the aforementioned Pathermuthis and Anatolios, through this our written contract of sale, of our own free will and with voluntary intent and irrevocable and sincere resolution, with steadfast conscience, with correct intention, without any fraud or intimidation or violence or deceit or constraint or any bad faith or deception, that we have sold to you, the aforementioned most well-born Isidora, and that we have devised to you with all the most complete right of lawful ownership and with good faith and with full authority and perpetual possession in accordance with every species of ownership, by means of this unique written sale, from now in perpetuity the girl who belongs to us and who has come to us by right of . . . from the other slave-traders of the Aithiopians,[22] the black[23] slave, Atalous by name, now renamed by you Eutukhia, about twelve years old more or less, an Aloan by race,[24] which afore-mentioned black slave not being previously mortgaged for any principal sum whatsoever or for any business or agreement or afflicted by any old injury or leprosy or beating or concealed ailment, but being free from all principal sum and business and agreement and of any old injury whatsoever and of any leprosy and of any beating and of any hidden ailment, for the mutually agreed, approved, resolved between us, full and just price for this same black slave, Atalous by name, now renamed by Eutukhia, an Aloan by race, about twelve years old more or less, four gold solidi,[25] of full weight, on the Alexandrian standard, making four gold solidi, of full weight, on the Alexandrian standard, which aforementioned price at once we, the venders, Pathermuthis and Anatolios, have been paid by you the afore-mentioned most well-born Isidora, from your hands into my hands, in full, in the sight of the witnesses who have subscribed in order below, having seen and confirmed their receipt, for her the slave to belong to you, the purchaser, the most well-born Isidora and to your testamentary heirs and successors and legal heirs, the afore-mentioned black female slave together with those offspring who, with God willing, shall be born of her, henceforth, already, or from this very day, which is the twenty-first of Thoth of the current third indiction, and from the day itself, continuously, perpetually, for you to possess and to control and to own with every right of ownership, to acquire, to possess, to use her and, with God willing, her children, to manage and to administer concerning her, to sell, to put up as security, to give away, to exchange as dowry and to give...and to give to your children and descendants, to leave behind and to transmit to your testamentary heirs, successors, and legal heirs, and in general to do and perform with her all such acts as the laws enjoin upon absolute owners to do with their own property, unhindered and unimpeded, from now for ever, this perpetual warranty and clearance of title and defense of the present sale in regard to every warranty falling on us, the venders.

And we further undertake that neither we nor anyone else on our behalf will proceed or defend ourselves against you, the purchaser, the well-born Isidora, and your testamentary heirs and successors and legal heirs, concerning any matter relating to this sale in any manner whatsoever.

25.

Axum in the Sixth Century C.E.

Despite the drama of the Christianization of Nubia, geography dictated that the later Roman Emperors would seek the alliance of Axum and not the Nubian kingdoms in their struggle with Sassanid Persia for hegemony in the Red Sea basin. This summary of the lost memoir of Nonnosus, a member of a family that had served the Roman Empire as ambassadors to the peoples of the Red Sea for three generations, provides a revealing glimpse into the complicated politics of the region and a clear idea of the extent of Roman knowledge of Axum during the reign of Justinian I (527–565 C.E.). Particularly noteworthy is Nonnosus' connection of the monsoon rains in the highlands of Ethiopia with the Nile flood, the most accurate account of the causes of the flood to be found in any classical writer.

Read[26] the History of Nonnosus, containing a description of his embassy to the Ethiopians,[27] Himyarites, and Saracens, then a most powerful nation, as well as to other Eastern peoples.[28] At this time Justinian (527–565 C.E.) was emperor of the Romans, and Qays chief of the Saracens.[29] This Qays was the grandson of Arethas, himself, a chief, to whom Nonnosus's grandfather was sent as ambassador, during the reign of Anastasius (491–518 C.E.),[30] to conclude a treaty of peace. Nonnosus's father Abrames had in like manner been sent on an embassy to Alamundarus,[31] chief of the Saracens, during the reign of Justin I (518–527 C.E.),[32] and was successful in procuring the release of Timostratus and John, two Roman generals who were prisoners of war. Qays, to whom Nonnosus was sent, was chief of two of the most illustrious Saracen tribes, the Kindites and Maadeni. Before Nonnosus was appointed ambassador, his father had been sent to this same Qays by Justinian, and had concluded a treaty of peace, on condition that Qays's son Mavias should be taken as a hostage to Byzantium.[33] After this, Nonnosus was entrusted with a threefold mission: to Qays, to induce him, if possible, to visit the emperor, to Elesbaas, king of the Axumites,[34] and then to the Himyarites.

Axum is a very large city, and may be considered the capital of Ethiopia; it lies more south and east than the Roman empire. Nonnosus, in spite of the treacherous attacks of tribesmen, perils from wild beasts, and many difficulties and dangers on the journey, successfully accomplished his mission, and returned in safety to his native land.

He relates that Qays, after Abrames had been sent to him a second time, set out for Byzantium, having previously divided his chieftaincy between his brothers Ambrus and Yezid. He brought a large number of his subjects with him, and was appointed administrator of Palestine by the emperor . . . .

He tells us that most of the Saracens, those who live in Phoenicon as well as beyond it and the Taurenian mountains, have a sacred meeting-place consecrated to one of the gods, where they assemble twice a year. One of these meetings lasts a whole month, almost to the middle of spring when the sun enters Taurus; the other lasts two months, and is held after the summer solstice. During these meetings complete peace prevails, not only amongst themselves, but also with all the natives; even the animals are at peace both with themselves and with human beings. Other strange, more or less fabulous information is also given.

He tells us that Adulis is fifteen days' journey from Axum. On his way there he and his companions saw a remarkable sight in the neighborhood of Aue,[35] midway between Axum and Adulis; this was a large number of elephants, nearly 5000. They were feeding in a large plain, and the inhabitants found it difficult to approach them or drive them from their pasture. This was what they saw on their journey.

We must also say something about the climatic contrarieties of summer and winter between Aue and Axum. When the sun enters Cancer, Leo, and Virgo, it is summer as far as Aue, as with us, and the atmosphere is extremely dry; but from Aue to Axum and the rest of Ethiopia, it is severe winter, not throughout the day, but beginning from midday, the sky being covered with clouds and the country flooded with violent rains. At that time also the Nile, spreading over Egypt, overflows and irrigates the land. But when the sun enters Capricornus, Aquarius, and Pisces,[36] the atmosphere, conversely, floods the country of the Adulites as far as Aue, while it is summer from Aue to Axum and the rest of Ethiopia, and the fruits of the earth are ripe.

During his voyage from Pharsan, Nonnosus, on reaching the last of the islands,[37] had a remarkable experience. He saw there certain creatures of human shape and form, very short, black-skinned, their bodies entirely covered with hair. The men were accompanied by women of the same appearance, and by boys still shorter. All were naked, women as well as men, except for a short apron of skin round their loins. There was nothing wild or savage about them. Their speech was human, but their language was unintelligible even to their neighbors, and still more so to Nonnosus and his companions. They live on shell-fish and fish cast up on the shore. According to Nonnosus, they were very timid, and when they saw him and his companions, they shrank from them as we do from monstrous wild beasts.

26.

Meeting with a King of Axum

In 530/31 C.E. Justinian I attempted to enlist the aid of the contemporary Axumite king Kaleb in a war against the South Arabian ruler Dhu Nuwas, who had converted to Judaism and was alleged to be persecuting the Christian inhabitants of his realm. In this excerpt from his report the Roman ambassador Julian provides a unique and vivid description of an Axumite king dressed in his full royal regalia.

In the same year,[38] the Romans and Persians broke their peace. The Persian war was renewed because of the embassy of the Homeritan Indians (Himyarite Arabs) to the Romans. The Romans sent the Magistrianos[39] Julian[40] from Alexandria down the Nile River and through the Indian Ocean[41] with sacral letters to Arethas, the king of the Ethiopians.[42] King Arethas[43] received him with great joy, since Arethas longed after the Roman Emperor's friendship.

On his return (to Constantinople), this same Julian reported that King Arethas was naked when he received him but had round his kidneys a loincloth of lien and gold thread. On his belly he wore linen with precious pearls; his bracelets had five spikes, and he wore gold armlets by his hands. He had a linen-and-gold cloth turban round his head, with four cords hanging down from both its straps.

He stood on (a carriage drawn by) four standing elephants

which had a yoke and four wheels. Like any stately carriage, it was ornamented with golden petals, just as are the carriages of provincial governors. While he stood upon it, he held in his hands a small gilded shield and two gold javelins. His counselors were all armed, and sang musical tunes.

When the Roman ambassador was brought in and had performed the prostration, he was ordered to rise by the king and was led before him. Arethas accepted the Emperor's sacral letters and tenderly kissed the seal which had the Emperor's image. He also accepted Julian's gifts and greatly rejoiced.

When he read the letter, he found that it was urgent for him to arm himself against the Persian king, devastate Persian territory near him, and in the future no longer make covenants with the Persian. Rather, the letter arranged that the land of the Homeritai would conduct its business with Egyptian Alexandria by way of the Nile River.[44]

In the sight of the envoy, King Arethas immediately began to campaign: he set war in motion against the Persians and sent out his Saracens. He himself also went off against Persian territory and pillaged all of it in that area. After conquering, King Arethas gave Julian a kiss of peace on the head and sent him off with a large retinue and many gifts.

27.

Letter from the Governor of Egypt to the King of the United Kingdom of Makouria and Nobatia (759 C.E.)

The end of antiquity in Egypt occurred in 642 C.E. when Arab invaders conquered Egypt and incorporated it into a new Islamic empire that extended from North Africa deep into Central Asia. Only in Nubia were the hitherto invincible Arab forces halted. In 652 C.E. an invading army from Egypt suffered a severe defeat trying to capture the Makourian capital of Dongola. As a result of that defeat, a peace treaty was concluded between Islamic Egypt and the united kingdom of Makouria and Nobatia. That treaty, known as the baqt *or "agreement," guaranteed the independence of Nubia if the Nubians would fulfill certain specified obligations: free passage for Moslems through Nubia, return of runaway slaves and subjects to Egypt, permission to establish a mosque in Dongola for the benefit of Muslim visitors, and the provision of a certain number of slaves to Egypt annually. Despite intervals of hostility, the* baqt *regulated relations between Egypt and Nubia for most of the Middle Ages and facilitated the survival of Christian states and culture in Nubia for almost a thousand years. The Arabic letter translated below was discovered at the important Nubian fortress of Qasr Ibrim and gives a unique insight into the role played by the* baqt *in relations between Nubia and Egypt in the eighth century* C.E.

In the name of God the Compassionate, the Merciful. From Musa b. K(?). . . [to] . . . master of Muqurra and Nubia. Peace be upon the friends of God and those who obey him . . . . To them do I praise God, other than whom there is no god.

To continue. You know that about which an agreement was made with you and the fulfillment of it which you took upon yourselves, so preserving your blood and property if you fulfill it.

God, blessed and exalted is he, says in His book 'Fulfill the compact of God when you make a compact, and do not break the oath after it has been affirmed and you have made God your guarantor; verily God knows what you do.' And he said 'Fulfill my compact and I shall fulfill your compact and mine; so fear me.' We have fulfilled for you that which we took upon ourselves for you in turning away from your blood and your property and you know your security in our land and your dwelling wherever you wish in it and the repairing of your merchants to us; no oppression or harm comes to them from us; no one of you who is among us is attacked by us nor is he denied his right; no obstacle is placed between your merchants and what they want—they are safe and contented wherever they go in our land, this being in fulfillment of our compact, in truth to our word, in belief in our Lord and in trust to our Prophet.[45]

You, however, in that which lies between us, behave otherwise. You do not bring to us that to which you are liable according to the *baqt*[46] on the basis of which agreement was made with you; nor do you return those of our slaves who run away to you; nor are our merchants safe among you; nor do you hasten to permit our messengers to return to us. You know that the people of all religions and the persuasions which neither know a lord, nor believe in a resurrection, nor hope for recompense, nor fear punishment, even these do not attack a merchant or detain a messenger. You make manifest to the people of your persuasion belief in Him who created the heavens and the earth and what is between them, you believe in Jesus the son of Mary and his book, and you make manifest to them justice and the doing of what is right, while what you do in that which is between you and us is contrary to that which you make manifest.

One of the merchants of the people of our country, Sa'd by name, came to you with much wealth, having made off with it from its owners, and you detained him among you, stood between him and the one who rightly pursued him and protected him from him. Secondly, a man of the people of Aswan, named Muhammad b. Zayd, sent to you a merchant of his, on his business and seeking rights for him. You detained him and the wealth that he had with him, and my governor over Aswan wrote to me, mentioning that he had written to your deputy[47] concerning him and that your deputy had written to him, asking him to send to him Muhammed b. Zayd, the master of that merchant, so that he might make over to him with the wealth which the merchant had with him. So the governor sent Muhammad to the deputy with a group of Muslims, and the deputy gave Muhammad a bad beating and broke his hand and detained him for three nights until Muhammad thought that he would kill him. Then the deputy let him go, and my governor over Aswan, Salm b. Sulayman, asked Muhammed for evidence of the arrival of his merchant to you and of that which your deputy had done to him.

Muhammad then brought to him a group of Muslims, witnesses of probity from the inhabitants of Aswan, and they bore witness to Salm of what Muhammad had mentioned in the matter of himself and the matter of his merchant. Salm then wrote to me about all of this and sent to me Muhammad b. Zayd, the master of that merchant. He came at the time of the arrival of Peter, your messenger to me, so I brought them together. With Peter was a group of your persuasion, and they mentioned that they thought when they took the merchant, that he was one of the Beja[48] who make attacks on them.

I then instructed 'Awn b. Sulayman, *qadi* of the people of Misr, to look into their affair; then were you made to bear the like of the right and justice which the people are made to bear, for he judged that Peter should return that merchant, together with the wealth that is with him, if he is alive, and if he is dead, you are liable to blood money of one thousand dinars.

Salm sent to you a messenger of his nine months ago, and a messenger four months ago, and you detained them, together with those slaves of the people of Islam and of the people protected by us who are with you, as well being liable to that which you are liable in the *baqt*. It is has been mentioned to me that you are liable to the *baqt* of [several?] years, which you have not fulfilled; as for that which have sent in accordance with the *baqt*, you have sent that in which there is no good—the one-eyed, or the lame, or the weak old man, or the young boy.[49]

So look into that about which I have written to you and hasten the dispatching to us of your remaining liability according to the *baqt* for the years for which you owe and do not send that in which there is no good, for we do not accept it; and send to us the merchant of Muhammad b. Zayd and the wealth which was with him, unless he has been killed, in which case send the thousand dinars, his blood money, together with the wealth which was with him; and send to us Sa'd the merchant who is among you and be not tardy in that in any respect if you wish us to fulfill for you our compact and to continue as we did in dealing correctly with you. Hasten that and do not delay it. If you do not obey, I shall have my view concerning what is between you and me, God willing. I have wanted to exceed the usual bounds in exhorting you and to take proof against you. Peace be upon the friends of God and those who obey him.

Written by Maymun on Sunday, the twelfth night remaining in Rajab in the year 141.[50]

NOTES

Notes to Introduction (p. 1–22)

1. The literature on this debate is enormous. For a brief overview see Stanley M. Burstein, "The Debate over *Black Athena*," *Scholia: Natal Studies in Classical Antiquity* 5 (1996): 3–16.
2. The material on Kush is adapted from my article "Introducing Kush: A Mini-Guide to an Ancient African Civilization," *Social Studies Review* 23 (1993): 22–30, by permission of the editor of *Social Studies Review*.
3. "Aithiopia" was identified with the territory of the modern country of Ethiopia by Christian writers after the conversion to Christianity of the Axumite king Ezana in the mid-fourth century C.E. in order to link it to the various Biblical references to "Aithiopia" (=Kush). For purposes of clarity the Greek spelling "Aithiopia" is preserved in texts referring to the Upper Nile valley, while "Ethiopia" is used for the modern country of that name.
4. The classic source for the "Solomonic" tradition about Axum is the *Kebra Nagast* ("The Glory of Kings"). For a translation of this fundamental work of Ethiopian culture see E. A. W. Budge, *The Queen of Sheba and her only son Menyelek (I)* (London, 1932).
5. In particular, spellings of proper names have been standardized. Supplements to texts are enclosed in carets, restored words in brackets, and explanatory words or phrases in parentheses. Dates are indicated as B.C.E. or C.E. Translations are by the editor unless otherwise specified.

Notes to Document 1 (p. 25–28)

Sources: Strabo, *Geography* 17.1.5, translated by H. C. Hamilton and W. Falconer, *The Geography of Strabo*, 3 vols. (London, 1857); and Diodorus, *Library of History* 1.37.

1. Modern Yemen and southern Arabia.
2. Legendary Egyptian king and conqueror, whose exploits were based loosely on those of several kings of the Twelfth Dynasty (1991–1785 B.C.E.). The most important ancient acount of Sesostris is found in Herodotus (*Histories* 2.102–110).

3. Cambyses invaded Nubia in 525 B.C.E. According to Herodotus (*Histories* 3.17–25), Cambyses turned back to Egypt after advancing only a short distance into Nubia. Persian inscriptions, however, suggest that Kush retained its independence while recognizing Persian suzerainty in the period after Cambyses' invasion (cf. Burstein, *Graeco-Africana: Studies in the History of Greek Relations with Egypt and Nubia* [New Rochelle, 1995], 155–164).

4. Greek historians and mythographers who wrote in the early and mid-fifth century B.C.E. Only fragments—quotations or references in other writers—survive, but these suggest that they located the source of the Nile in Ocean, the great body of water believed by early Greeks to surround the world's land masses (cf. Truesdell S. Brown, *The Greek Historians* [Lexington: 1973], 1–23).

5. Greek historians of the fifth and fourth centuries B.C.E.

6. Ptolemy II campaigned in Nubia in the 270s B.C.E. As a result of his campaign, Ptolemaic Egypt annexed the Dodecaschoenus, the seventy-mile stretch of the Nile Valley immediately south of the First Cataract, together with the gold mines in the desert east of the Nile described in Document 3.

7. The reference is to *Nun*, the primordial waters that the Egyptians believed were the source of creation and the Nile and that Greek thinkers identified with Ocean.

8. For these people see Document 6.

9. This has been shown to be a correct Greek interpretation of an ancient Nubian term (cf. Burstein, *Agatharchides*, 90 n. 4).

Notes to Document 2 (p. 29–30)

Source: Strabo, *Geography* 17.1.2. Translated by H. C. Hamilton and W. Falconer, *The Geography of Strabo*, 3 vols. (London, 1857).

10. Eight stades equals one mile.

11. In Greek geographical terminology Libya designates Africa west of the Nile.

12. The Atbara River, which joins the Nile about 80 miles north of Meroë.

13. There is some confusion in Eratosthenes' account at this point. The Astapous is the White Nile, which flows north from Lake Victoria in Uganda and joins the Blue Nile at Khartoum to form the main body of the Nile. The Astasobas may be either the Blue Nile or another smaller tributary of the Nile called the Sobat which joins the White Nile south of

Khartoum.

14. Actually, it is the swelling of the Blue Nile as a result of the summer monsoon that causes the Nile to flood.

15. The reference is to the Gezira, which, like the island of Meroë, is not a true island but a triangular area of land bounded on two sides by rivers, namely, the White and Blue Niles. The Sembritae are supposed to be the descendants of mutineers (cf. Herodotus, *Histories* 2.30), who abandoned their posts at Syene (=Aswan) and fled into Nubia during the reign of the Egyptian king Psamtek I, the founder of the Twenty-sixth Dynasty (664–610 B.C.E.).

16. For the Blemmyes see Documents 13, 16, 21–22.

17. For the Trogodytes see Document 6.

18. For the Nubae see Documents 13, 21–23.

Notes to Document 3 (p. 31–34)

Source: Reprinted from Agatharchides of Cnidus, *On the Erythraean Sea*, translated by Stanley M. Burstein (London, 1989), Fragments 23–29, by permission of the Hakluyt Society.

19. The mines in question are in the Wadi Allaqi and Wadi Gabgaba, a complex network of ancient dry river-beds that leave the Nile Valley near the southern end of the Dodecaschoenus and run southeastward toward the Red Sea. For ancient gold mining in Nubia in general see J. Vercoutter, "The Gold of Kush," *Kush* 7 (1959): 120–153.

20. The Ptolemies, the Macedonian dynasty that ruled Egypt from the death of Alexander the Great in 323 B.C.E. until the Roman conquest of Egypt in 30 B.C.E.

21. The process is called fire-setting and involves setting fires against a rock face, and then fracturing the rock by quickly quenching the heated surface with cold water or vinegar.

22. The Wadi Allaqi and Wadi Gabgaba were the principal gold mining regions in Lower Nubia. Mining activity in this area—called Wawat in Egyptian texts—is first attested during the Egyptian Middle Kingdom (ca. 1900 B.C.E.). There is no evidence to substantiate Agatharchides' claim that mining was suspended during the periods of Aithiopian—Twenty-fifth Dynasty—and Persian rule in Egypt. If true, however, it would suggest that the mines were first reopened after the Macedonian conquest of Egypt in the late 330s B.C.E.

Notes to Document 4 (p. 35–36)

Source: Diodorus, *Library of History* 1.33, with supplements from Strabo, *Geography* 17.2.2.

23. The ultimate source of this description of Meroë was an extensive account of the Nile River that was included in the second book of the lost *On Affairs in Asia* written by the second century B.C.E. historian Agatharchides of Cnidus. Independent summaries of this passage were made by two first century B.C.E. writers, the historian Diodorus of Agyrium and the geographer Artemidorus of Ephesus, the latter of whose summary survives in the *Geography* of the first century C.E. geographer Strabo.
24. Strabo's description is not clear as it stands. The Island of Meroë is formed by the junction north of the city of Meroë of two northward flowing rivers, the Nile (=Astapous) and the Astaboras (=Atbara). For ancient knowledge of the geography of this region see Document 2.
25. Probably Lake Tana.

Notes to Document 5 (p. 37–46)

Sources: Diodorus, *Library of History* 3.2–10, with supplements from Strabo, *Geography* 17.2.2.

26. See Document 1.
27. Sammuramat, the Babylonian wife of the Assyrian king Shamshi-Adad V (823–811 B.C.E.), to whom Greek historians ascribed conquests comparable to those of Cyrus I of Persia and Alexander the Great (cf. Martin Braun, *History and Romance in Graeco-Oriental Literature* [Oxford, 1938], 6–12). For an account of her Aithiopian campaign, see Diodorus 2.14–15.
28. Diodorus' source apparently claimed "Aithiopian," that is, Meroitic, authority for the view that Egyptian civilization originated in Nubia. The ancient evidence for this theory is discussed in Stanley M. Burstein, "The Origins of the Napatan State in Classical Sources," *Graeco-Africana*, 29–39.
29. Actually, the Egyptians used three scripts: Hieroglyphic, which was used in the first millennium B.C.E. primarily for monumental inscriptions; Demotic, a cursive script that used extremely abbreviated forms of the hieroglyphic symbols and was employed primarily for economic and legal texts; and Hieratic, a simplified form of the hieroglyphic script used primarily for writing books. Since Hieratic was used only for the copying

of religious texts in the Hellenistic Period, Greek writers were unlikely to have encountered it. The Kushites employed the Hieroglyphic script for monumental and religious inscriptions until they invented an alphabet to write their own language in the late third or early second century B.C.E.

30. The *Was* scepter which consisted of a shaft, a handle shaped like the head of a canine, and a base ending in two prongs. In Egypt it was primarily used in funerary contexts (cf. Ian Shaw and Paul Nicholson, *The Dictionary of Ancient Egypt* [London, 1995], 304).

31. The so-called White Crown, which Egyptian kings wore in their capacity as rulers of southern or Upper Egypt.

32. The Uraeus, sacred animal of Wadjyt, goddess of Buto, who was believed to protect the king. Unlike Egyptian kings, the kings of Kush wore two Uraei instead of one.

33. Amun.

34. Kushite texts, such as the so-called "Election Stela of Aspelta," indicate that the role of the divine oracle was not to choose a new king but to give public legitimacy to a particular candidate who had already been designated for the throne (cf. *Fontes Historiae Nubiorum*, edited by T. Eide, T. Hägg, R. H. Pierce, and L. Török, Vol. 1 [Bergen, 1994], 244–248).

35. Ergamenes is the only Meroitic king mentioned by name in classical literature and is most probably to be identified with Arkamani-qo (ca. 270–260 B.C.E.), the first king to build a pyramid and be buried at Meroë instead of Napata. There is no other evidence for the custom of royal suicide. The close ties with Ptolemaic Egypt implied by the reference to the king's Greek education are reflected also in the large number of Mediterranean luxury goods found in Meroitic royal and noble tombs. Relations between Meroë and Ptolemaic Egypt are discussed in L. Török, "Kush and the External World," *Meroitica* 10 (1989): 47–217; and Stanley M. Burstein, "The Hellenistic Fringe," *Graeco-Africana*, 105–123.

36. Although there is no evidence to support the story that Meroitic courtiers deliberately mutilated themselves in order to mimic the deformities of their king, retainer sacrifice is a well-attested feature of Meroitic and post-Meroitic royal burials; cf. William Y. Adams, *Nubia: Corridor to Africa* (Princeton, 1977), 308–309 and 409.

37. Arabia refers to the area east of the Nile and not the Arabian Peninsula.

38. For these supplements see Document 4, note 1.

39. For these peoples see Documents 6 and 7.

40. Zeus is to be identified with Amun. Heracles may refer to the Meroitic war god Apedemak whose lion head might have suggested to Greeks the lion-skin cap supposedly worn by Heracles. What Meroitic deity is to be

identified with Pan is unknown.

41. Stories of elephant-eating snakes were popular in antiquity. Fragments of a painting with such a theme were, in fact, discovered at Meroë early in the twentieth century.

Notes to Document 6 (p. 47–50)

Source: Reprinted from Agatharchides of Cnidus, *On the Erythraean Sea*, translated by Stanley M. Burstein (London, 1989), Fragments 62–64, by permission of the Hakluyt Society.

42. As is indicated by the reference to "Trogodytes called Megabari," "Trogodyte" is an umbrella term for various groups of transhumant pastoralists who inhabited the eastern deserts and Red Sea hills and whom historians identify with the Blemmyes and Beja of late ancient and medieval Nubia. The actual meaning of the term is unknown. It was early corrupted by Greek writers into "Troglodyte," "Cave-Dwellers," although there is no evidence that any of these peoples ever primarily lived in caves.

43. In Greek and Roman geographical and ethnographic texts "tyrant" designates a local chief subordinate to an overlord.

44. The various aspects of the life-style described in this text such as blood-drinking, strong identification with a people's domesticated animals, and the existence of pariah groups such as butchers are all characteristic features of the cultures of transhumant pastoralists in medieval and modern northeast Africa (cf. E. E. Evans-Pritchard, *The Nuer* [Oxford, 1940]; and George Peter Murdock, *Africa: Its Peoples and their Culture History* [New York, 1959], 193–203).

45. Strong seasonal winds that blow steadily from the north beginning about July and continuing throughout the summer.

46. The specific nature of the genital mutilation intended is not clear, although some of the groups in this area do excise one of a male's testicles.

Notes to Document 7 (p. 51–52)

Source: Reprinted from Agatharchides of Cnidus, *On the Erythraean Sea*, translated by Stanley M. Burstein (London, 1989), by permission of the Hakluyt Society.

47. I.e. "Snub-nosed People."

48. The "Ostrich Eaters" are one of a number of hunter-gathering peoples Agatharchides located in the steppes and marsh lands south and east of Meroë. The exact location of this particular group is unclear. So also is their existence as a distinct ethnic group since, as the term "Ostrich-Eaters" indicates, Greek explorers attempted to distinguish peoples on the basis of their primary food source without considering the possibility that one people might exploit several different food sources as the occasion required.

Notes to Document 8 (p. 55–56)

Source: Étienne Bernand, *Les Inscriptions Grecques et Latines de Philae*, vol. 2 (Paris, 1969), 127 (Latin version).

1. Roman poet and soldier (ca. 69–26 B.C.E.). Gallus committed suicide after being recalled to Rome because of charges that he had exceeded his authority by setting up monuments in royal style in his own honor.

2. The highest official in Roman Egypt. The post was always held by an equestrian, an upper-class Roman who chose not to pursue a political career that might result in admission to the Senate. Under Augustus and his successors equestrians served primarily in financial posts in the provinces and governed several provinces of which Egypt was the most important.

3. Augustus (63 B.C.E.–14 C.E.). The "god" refers to Julius Caesar who was deified by the Roman Senate after his assassination in 44 B.C.E.

4. Pharaonic Egypt was divided into forty-two districts called *nomes*. The Thebaïd consisted of the seven nomes of Upper Egypt from Thebes to the First Cataract at Aswan. Under the Ptolemies they formed a special administrative unit governed by an *Epistrategos*, a military official with both military and civil powers.

5. This is an exaggeration since the Ptolemies, like the Persians and their Pharaonic predecessors, had governed Lower Nubia.

6. Beginning in the late third century B.C.E. there had been repeated rebellions centered in the Thebaïd, the last of which, in 88 B.C.E., had resulted in severe damage to the city of Thebes.

7. Lower Nubia from the First to the Second Cataract.

8. The monument consists of a large stele of rose-colored granite bearing a relief of a cavalryman victorious over a prostrate enemy and an inscription in Egyptian hieroglyphs, Latin, and Greek commemorating Gallus'

victories. The Greek text is a loose translation of the Latin version. The Egyptian text has never been properly published. The monument was cut in two and used for as building material after Gallus' disgrace.

Notes to Document 9 (p. 57–61)

Source: Strabo, *Geography* 17.1.54. Based on the translation by H. C. Hamilton and W. Falconer, *The Geography of Strabo*, 3 vols. (London, 1857).

9. Syene is modern Aswan. For these peoples see Document 2.
10. See Document 8.
11. Gaius Petronius, Prefect of Egypt from 25 to 21 B.C.E.
12. The reference is to an unsuccessful attempt in 26 B.C.E. to conquer the Kingdom of Saba in modern Yemen by Aelius Gallus, Prefect of Egypt from 27 to 25 B.C.E.; for a brief account of this campaign see G. W. Bowersock, *Roman Arabia* (Cambridge, MA, 1983), 46–49.
13. Modern Dakka near the southern end of the Dodecaschoenus.
14. In Pharaonic Egypt the *nomarchs* were the chief administrative officers of the forty-two *nomes* into which Egypt was divided. Their authority was steadily reduced in the Hellenistic Period and in the Roman Period they were primarily fiscal officials.
15. Modern Qasr Ibrim, an important fortified center just north of Abu Simbel.
16. According to Herodotus (3.17–25) the Persian king Cambyses unsuccessfully attempted to invade Kush ca. 525 B.C.E. As Kush appears to have recognized Persian suzerainty, the extent of Cambyses' failure has probably been exaggerated in the sources; cf. Stanley M. Burstein, "Herodotus and the Emergence of Meroë," *Graeco-Africana*, 165–173.
17. Candace was the title of the mother of the Meroitic king. During the late first century B.C.E. and first half of the first century C.E. several Candaces appear to have functioned as ruling queens. Strabo's claim that Napata was a royal residence in the late first century B.C.E. is confirmed by the presence of a number of royal pyramids dated to this period built in the old royal cemetery at Nuri.
18. Apparently not all of them were returned since a splendid bronze head most probably from one of these statues was discovered in Meroë early in the twentieth century.
19. A people in Northwest Spain conquered by Augustus in the late 20s B.C.E.
20. The reference to the remission of tribute implies that Kush had become subject to Rome prior to the outbreak of the hostilities described in this text; cf. Document 8.

Notes to Document 10 (p. 62–65)

Source: Pliny, *Historia Naturalis* 6.181–186. Translated by John Bostock and H. T. Riley, *The Natural History of Pliny*, Vol. 2 (London, 1855).

21. The reference is to several lists of settlements on both sides of the Nile in Nubia excerpted by Pliny (*HN* 6.177–180) from several Hellenistic accounts of Aithiopia.
22. Members of the Praetorian guard, the elite troops that served as the emperor's personal guard.
23. See Document 9.
24. The second cataract.
25. Pliny has reconstructed an "ancient Aithiopian" empire on the basis of references to Aithiopia in two Greek legends, namely, that of Memnon, who supposedly fought on the Trojan side late in the Trojan War, and that of Perseus and Andromeda, which was traditionally located at Byblos in Phoenicia. The flaw in Pliny's reasoning is that in early Greek geographical thought Aithiopia designated the entire southern portion of the world and was only secondarily restricted to Africa. Legendary figures from the east such as Memnon, whose original home was supposed to be Susa in southeastern Iran, could therefore be said to come from "Aithiopia"; cf. O. A. W. Dilke, *Greek and Roman Maps* (London, 1985), 27.
26. All of these writers probably lived during the third century B.C.E.
27. For Eratosthenes and Artemidorus see Documents 2 and 4. All that is known about Sebosus Statius is that he wrote about Africa and India in the late Hellenistic Period or early first century C.E.
28. A slightly different account of this expedition is preserved in Seneca, *Naturales Quaestiones* 6.8.3–4.
29. I.e. Baboons.
30. This is exaggerated. Ruling queens are attested only in the first century B.C.E. and the first and early fourth centuries C.E.
31. The temple of Amon at Meroë was excavated early in the twentieth century.
32. The reference is probably to district chiefs, who recognized the authority of the ruler of Meroë. For an example of such a district ruler see Document 2. It is likely that the ruler of Meroë was more of a paramount chief in a confederation of district chieftains than the head of a centralized bureaucratic state.

Notes to Document 11 (p. 66–68)

Source: É. Bernand, *Inscriptions Métriques de l'Égypte Gréco-Romaine* (Paris, 1968), No. 168.

33. The poem has a simple tripartite structure. The first section (lines 1–28) is an autobiographical account of the origin of the poem; the second section (lines 29–32) is a brief hymn celebrating the power and gifts of Mandulis; the third section (lines 33–36) refers to Mandulis' order that the poem be inscribed on the walls of Kalabsha temple and, apparently, to the acrostic in which Paccius Maximus concealed his signature.
34. I.e. Kalabsha temple.
35. The allusion is most likely to Paccius Maximus' native language and suggests that he was, at least, partially of "Nubian" origin.
36. The parallel with Mandulis, who is known to be a sun god, suggests that Breith is to be identified with the moon.
37. The reference is to an acrostic composed of the initial letters of the first twenty-three lines: "I, Paccius Maximus, a *decurion*, wrote it." A *decurion* was the commander of a ten-man squad in an auxiliary cavalry unit.

Notes to Document 12 (p. 69–72)

Source: F. Ll. Griffith, *Catalogue of the Demotic Graffiti of the Dodecaschoenus*, Vol. 1 (Oxford, 1937), Ph. 416, with corrections by Professor A. Lopreino.

38. The exact meanings of the titles *qeren* and *qeren-akrere* are unknown, although they appear to refer to administrative offices of some kind.
39. Literally the "untrodden place." The reference is to Bigah Island near Philae, which was believed to be the location of the tomb of Osiris.
40. A talent could refer either to the highest unit in Greek monetary systems or to a weight. In the latter case, a talent equaled approximately fifty-two pounds. Unfortunately, it is not clear if Pasan was referring to ten talents of silver or to an amount of silver valued at ten talents.
41. The king of Kush.
42. One of the forty-two administrative districts into which Egypt was divided. The reference is to the southernmost nome, which included Philae.
43. The *pesto* or Meroitic royal governor of Lower Nubia. The title is ultimately derived from the old Egyptian title for the governor of Nubia, "King's Son of Kush," and like the latter expresses not the holder's actual kinship with the king but his being the king's viceroy in Lower Nubia.

44. September, 251 C.E. to August, 252 C.E.
45. October, 252 C.E.
46. Reigned ca. 246 C.E. to 266 C.E.
47. Beginning in the third century C.E. military affairs in Lower Nubia were divided between two officials, the "generals of the desert" and the "generals of the river." The offices appear to have been hereditary in a few noble families in the region.
48. Egyptian months were divided into three ten-day "weeks."
49. Osiris, the husband of Isis and god of the dead, here identified with the war god Onuris, whom Egyptian myth closely associated with Nubia.
50. From October/November, 252 C.E. to February/March, 253 C.E.
51. The area immediately in front of the pylon of the Temple of Isis, which was open to the public.
52. Kush took advantage of Roman weakness in the mid-third century C.E. to briefly extend its power to include the whole of Lower Nubia to the first cataract; cf. L. Török, *Late Antique Nubia: History and archaeology of the southern neighbour of Egypt in the 4th–6th c. A.D.* (Budapest, 1987), 25–26.
53. Abratoye was one of the principal Meroitic officials in Lower Nubia in the third century C.E., having held numerous priestly and military offices in Nubia before becoming *pesto* (cf. L. Török, *Economic Offices and Officials in Meroitic Nubia [A Study in Territorial Administration of the Late Meroitic Kingdom]* [Budapest, 1979], 5).
54. The total disappearance of a person's name entailed the loss of immortality in Egyptian thought.
55. Gaius Vibius Trebonianus Gallus was emperor from 251 to 253 C.E. His "son" was the son of his predecessor Decius whom he adopted.
56. March, 253 C.E.

Notes to Document 13 (p. 73–76)

Source: Procopius, *Persian War* 1.19.27–37. Reprinted from "Greek, Latin and Coptic Sources for Nubian History" by T. Eide, T. Hägg and R. H. Pierce, *Sudan Texts Bulletin* 2 (1980) 5–7, by permission of the translators.

57. Axum.
58. For this road, which bypassed the Nile Valley, see Document 15.
59. I.e. the eastern deserts of Egypt and Nubia. Historians identify the Blemmyes with the Bega or Beja of Axumite (cf. Documents 15 and 16) and Medieval Arabic sources and the nomadic Trogodytes whose customs are described in Document 6.

60. For the Nobatai (=Nubae) see Documents 21–23.

61. I.e. the Dodecaschoenus.

62. This is usually interpreted as a reference to Khargeh Oasis in the western desert of Egypt.

63. Procopius is in error here, since, as Document 21 reveals, the Nobatai only seized control of the Dodecaschoenus from the Blemmyes in the fifth century C.E.

64. I.e. they became *federatae*, barbarian tribes charged with the duty of defending Roman frontiers in return for subsidies and permission to settle on former Roman territory.

65. An island at the southern end of the First Cataract famous for its great temple of Isis built by Ptolemy II (283–246 B.C.E.). The origin of the name Philae is unknown. Procopius' claim that Diocletian named the island becase of his expectation of friendship between the Blemmyes, Nobatai and the Romans is erroneous since the name is already attested in the Hellenistic Period (cf. Diodorus, *Library of History* 1.22.3).

66. Cf. Document 22.

67. Constantinople.

Notes to Document 14 (p. 79–82)

Source: *Periplus of the Erythraean Sea* 1–6. Reprinted from Wilfred H. Schoff, *The Periplus of the Erythraean Sea* (New York, 1912) 1–6.

1. In antiquity the Erythraean Sea designated the Indian Ocean and its two gulfs, the Red Sea and the Persian Gulf.

2. Myos Hormos has now been identified with the Medieval and Egyptian port of Quseir al-Qadim.

3. I.e., 225 miles, assuming eight stades to the mile, which is almost exactly correct since the actual distance is 230 miles.

4. For the tendency of Greek explorers and geographers to name people according to their primary means of subsistence see Document 7, note 2. The fullest account of the Fish-Eaters is in Agatharchides of Cnidus, *On the Erythraean Sea*, Fragments 30–50.

5. Aqiq, near modern Port Sudan. Ptolemais of the Hunts was founded by Ptolemy II to serve as a base for launching expeditions to capture and bring back Elephants to be trained for war. The fullest account of Berenice and its archaeological remains is found in Steven Sidebotham and Willemina Wendrich, *Berenike '94: Preliminary Report of the Excavations at Berenike (Egyptian Red Sea Coast) and the Survey of the Eastern Desert*

(Leiden, 1995) and *Berenike '95: Preliminary Report of the Excavations at Berenike (Egyptian Red Sea Coast) and the Survey of the Eastern Desert* (Leiden, 1996).

6. Modern Massawa in Eritrea. 375 miles, a serious overestimate since the actual sea distance is 180 miles.

7. Two and a half miles.

8. The reference is probably to the region of Sennar in the Sudan, south of the junction of the White and Blue Niles at Khartoum.

9. For elephants near Axum and Adulis see Document 25. Overhunting of elephants for ivory in the Hellenistic and early Roman periods decimated the herds living in regions that were easily accessible from the coast of the Red Sea; cf. S. M. Burstein, "Ivory and Ptolemaic Exploration of the Red Sea: The Missing Factor," *Topoi* 6 (1996): 799–807.

10. The Dahlach Islands.

11. Zoscales is usually identified with an early Axumite king named Za-Haqâlê on the basis of the similarity of the names. No evidence exists, however, to confirm the correctness of the identification.

12. *Monache* and *sagmatogênê* clearly refer to types of Indian cotton cloth, but the exact significance of these terms is unclear.

13. For the articles in this list see Lionel Casson, *The Periplus Maris Erythraei* (Princeton, 1989), 110–114.

Notes to Document 15 (p. 83–86)

Source: *The Christian Topography of Cosmas, an Egyptian Monk*, translated by J. W. McCrindle (London, 1897), 59–66.

14. The beginning of the inscription, which would have contained the king's name and titles, unfortunately is lost. The king's references to Zeus, Ares, and Poseidon, however, indicates that the inscription is to be dated prior to the conversion of Axum to Christianity in the fourth century C.E.

15. The Gaze are the Axumites which suggests that the king came to power as the result of a rebellion or had to fight a civil war during his reign.

16 I.e. the Beja or Blemmyes.

17. Unfortunately, it is not possible to exactly determine the location of the various peoples the king claims to have conquered. Two broad areas can, however, be identified: one in Africa extending north to the borders of Egypt, west to the Meroitic frontier, and south toward Somalia and the mouth of the Red Sea; and a second in the western portion of the Arabian peninsula extending from Leuke Kome (=White Village) near the

entrance to the Gulf of Aqaba in the north to Yemen in the south.

18. The Axumite pantheon was South Arabian in origin. True to their Greek educations, the Auxmites identified their gods with the gods of the Greek pantheon, so Astar was identified with Zeus; Mahrem, the war-god and divine ancestor of the king, with Ares; and Beher with Poseidon. Astar's functions are unknown, but the fact that Astar/Zeus always holds the first place in Axumite god lists suggests that he was the head of the pantheon.

19. This inscription was originally inscribed on the back of a stone throne set up to commemorate the king's victories.

Notes to Document 16 (p. 87–88)

Source: Sir E. A. Wallis Budge, *A History of Ethiopia Nubia & Abyssinia*, Vol. 1 (London, 1928), 245–246.

20. The exact dates of Ezana's reign are unknown. Stuart Munro-Hay suggests (*Aksum: An African Civilization of Late Antiquity* [Edinburgh, 1991], 67) that he ruled from the 320s C.E. to the early 350s C.E. His description of himself as "son of Ares (=Mahrem) indicates that this inscription, of which versions are known in Greek, Ge'ez, and South Arabian, dates from the period before his conversion to Christianity in the 330s C.E.

21. Ezana's titulary shows that his empire included territories in both Africa and Arabia. Particularly interesting is his claim to be King of Kasu, that is, Kush, since it indicates that Axumite suzerainty over Kush already existed in the early years of his reign; cf. Stanley M. Burstein, "Axum and the Fall of Meroe," *Graeco-Africana*, 207–213.

22. The Bega had already been conquered by the unknown Axumite king whose exploits are celebrated in Document 15.

23. The location of Matlia is unknown. The reference to the Bega receiving four months provisions for the journey suggests that they were moved to a part of the kingdom far removed from their traditional home in the eastern desert and Red Sea hills.

24. As the title king of kings suggests, the Axumite empire had a quasi-federal character with the Axumite king ruling over a number of subkings or "kinglets" in Axumite terminology; cf. Munro-Hay, 160.

Notes to Document 17 (p. 89–90)

Source: Sir E. A. Wallis Budge, *A History of Ethiopia Nubia & Abyssinia*, Vol. 1 (London, 1928), 248–249.

25. The references to pagan gods date this inscription to the period before Ezana's conversion to Christianity.
26. Unfortunately, none of the places and peoples mentioned in this inscription can be located, so that it is impossible to reconstruct the course of Ezana's campaign or to identify the trade route followed by the caravan whose destruction provoked his actions.
27. Presumably they became slaves. For Axumite slave raiding see Document 18.
28. Apparently, an earth deity; cf. Munro-Hay, 196.
29. It is not clear if the cattle and prisoners became part of Mahrem's temple property or were sacrificed to him; cf. Munro-Hay, 198.

Notes to Document 18 (p. 91–93)

Source: *The Christian Topography of Cosmas, An Egyptian Monk,* translated by J. W. McCrindle (London, 1898), 52–54.

30. Apparently, Somalia, which would place Sasu in the southern portion of the Axumite empire.
31. Southwest of Axum near Lake Tana.
32. Herodotus (*Histories* 4.196) claims that the Carthaginians conducted similar "silent trade" trade with peoples living on the northwest coast of Africa in the fifth century B.C.E.
33. Cf. Document 17 for the danger to trade posed by tribal raiders.
34. I.e. from late June (=beginning of Epiphi, the eleventh month of the Egyptian year) to late August (=beginning of Thoth, the first month of the Egyptian year).

Notes to Document 19 (p. 94–96)

Source: Reprinted from A. H. M. Jones and Elizabeth Monroe, *A History of Abyssinia* (Oxford, 1935), 26–27, by permission of Oxford University Press.

35. With the decline of direct contact between India and the Mediterranean in Late Antiquity, the meaning of the geographical term "India" was broadened to include Northeast Africa and South Arabia, where Roman merchants obtained Indian goods from Axumite and South Arabian intermediaries. Often the exact location intended by a particular author can only be determined from context, so that in this instance "further India" apparently refers to Axum; cf. Philip Mayerson, "A Confusion of Indias:

Asian India and African India in the Byzantine Sources," *Journal of the American Oriental Society* 113 (1993): 171.

36. The king whom Frumentius and Aedesius served is probably to be identified with Ella Amida, the father of Ezana.

37. For an illuminating account of the important role played by merchants in spreading various religions in Late Antiquity and the Middle Ages, see Jerry H. Bentley, *Old World Encounters: Cross-Cultural Contacts and Exchanges in Pre-Modern Times* (Oxford, 1993).

38. In view of Frumentius' close ties to Athanasius, the reference is probably to the customs of the Alexandrian Christians.

39. Rufinus' chronology of Frumentius' career is vague. In fact, while Athanasius became bishop of Alexandria in 328 C.E., Frumentius was actually consecrated Bishop of Axum during the reign of the Roman emperor Constantius II, who ruled from 337 to 351 C.E.

40. Rufinus.

Notes to Document 20 (p. 97–100)

Source: Reprinted from L. P. Kirwan, "A Survey of Nubian Origins," *Sudan Notes and Records* 20 (1937): 50–51, by permission of the Royal Geographical Society.

41. In accordance with traditional Axumite practice Ezana set up inscriptions commemorating his campaign against in three languages: Greek, Ge'ez, and South Arabian. The text translated here is the Ge'ez version. Portions of the Greek and South Arabian versions have recently been discovered; cf. F. Anfray, A. Caquot, and P. Nautin, "Une nouvelle inscription grécque d'Ezana, Roi d'Axoum," *Journal des Savants* (1970): 260–273.

42. Ezana's invocation of the "Lord of Heaven" and the absence of references to the traditional Axumite deities suggested to scholars that this inscription dated from the period after Ezana's conversion to Christianity, a suggestion that has been confirmed by the overtly Christian character of the recently discovered Greek inscription dealing with these same events.

43. Probably the Atbara River.

44. According to the recently discovered Greek inscription dealing with these events (see note 41), Ezana's campaign was his response to appeals for aid against the Noba made to him by these peoples.

45. Probably the Nile.

46. This is the earliest reference to the use of riding camels in Nubia.

47. I.e. Kush. The distinction Ezana draws between the towns of the Noba

and Kasu suggests that Meroë and its immediate environs were still controlled by Kushites and not the Noba. The discovery at Meroë of two Greek inscriptions set up by pagan Axumite kings combined with the presence of "Kasu," Ezana's titulary, suggests that Meroë had become a vassal state of Axum some time prior to Ezana's campaign; cf. S. Burstein, "Axum and the Fall of Meroe," *Graeco-Africana*, 207–213.

48. It has been suggested that Alwa is to be identified with Meroë, but certainty is impossible. All that can said with confidence is that these towns were located somewhere in the Island of Meroë.

49. The basis for the distinction between Black and Red Noba is unknown.

Notes to Document 21 (p. 103–105)

Source: *Orientis Graeci Inscriptiones Selectae*, 2 vols. (Leipzig, 1903–1905), 201.

1. Silko's use of the title *Basiliskos*, "Kinglet," is puzzling since it implies subordination to a *Basileus*, "King," while Silko clearly claims supremacy over "Kings" in his inscription. The situation is made more complicated by the fact that Silko's successor is called a *Basileus* in a recently published letter addressed to him by a king of the Blemmyes (cf. J. Rea, "The Letter of Phonen to Aburni," *Zeitschrift für Papyrologie und Epigraphik* 34 [1979]: 152, line 1). No completely satisfactory solution to this problem has been found, but the most likely is the suggestion of Tomas Hägg ("Titles and Honorific Epithets in Nubian Greek Texts," *Symbolae Osloenses* 65 [1990]: 148–156) that Silko used the diminutive "Kinglet" in public documents that might come to the attention of Roman officials in Egypt for whom the only legitimate "King" was the Roman emperor.

2. The metaphor of Silko as a "bear" is puzzling since bears are not native to Northeast Africa. Presumably, the scribe responsible for the Greek text of Silko's inscription mistranslated a Nobatai term for a local animal.

3. I.e. from Qasr Ibrim in the south to Kalabsha in the north. The letter of the Blemmye king Phonen referred to in Note 1 indicates that the Nobatai continued to occupy this territory after the death of Silko.

4. I.e. in Upper Nubia south of Qasr Ibrim. Whether these Nobatai are to be identified with the Black and Red Noba of Ezana's inscription is unclear.

Notes to Document 22 (p. 106–107)

Source: Priscus Fragment 21. Reprinted from T. Eide, T. Hägg and R. H. Pierce, "Three Greek Texts," *Sudan Texts Bulletin* 1 (1979): 9–12, by permission of the translators.

5. Cf. Document 13 for the reverence of these peoples for Isis of Philae.

6. "Despot" (*tyrannos*) and "sub-despot" (*hypotyrannos*) are the terms used by the Romans to refer to either a tribal chieftain or a local headman subject to the overlordship of another ruler.

Notes to Document 23 (p. 108–117)

Source: John of Ephesus, *Ecclesiastical History* 4.6–4.53. Reprinted from *The Third Part of the Ecclesiastical History of John Bishop of Ephesus*, translated by R. Payne Smith (Oxford, 1860).

7. Theodosius was Patriarch of Alexandria from 535 to 566 C.E.

8. Cf. Document 13 for the payment of subsidies to the Nobatai and Blemmyes.

9. Theodora was a supporter of the doctrine of Monophysitism, that is, the teaching that Christ had only one divine nature. Monophysitism was espoused by the Coptic-speaking church in Egypt, although it had been condemned by the Council of Chalcedon in 451 C.E., which reaffirmed the view that Christ had both a human and divine nature. John's hostility to Chalcedonian doctrine is evident throughout his account.

10. The duke (*dux*) was the governor of the Thebaïd, the southernmost of the four provinces of Egypt under Justinian.

11. I.e. to the borders of Nobatia, the northernmost of the three kingdoms that occupied the territory of the former kingdom of Kush. Its territory extended from the First Cataract to the Third Cataract.

12. Theodosius was deposed as Patriarch of Alexandria by Justinian I on grounds of heresy in 536 C.E.

13. I.e. in the mid-550s C.E.

14. I..e. the ruler of the kingdom of Alwa which occupied the region from the Island of Meroë south to Sennar. Its capital was at Soba near the junction of the White and Blue Niles.

15. The inhabitants of the kingdom of Makouria, which extended from roughly the Third to the Fifth Cataract. The date of the conversion of Makouria to Chalcedonian Christianity is unknown, but it must have occurred before 572 C.E. since in that year Makourian ambassadors came to Constantinople bringing as gifts to the Emperor Justin II a number of elephant tusks and a giraffe (John of Biclaro, *Chronicle* 28).

16. I.e. The Red Sea.

17. Monophysitism, the doctrine that Christ had a single divine nature. This passage implies that Axumite missionaries were active in Upper Nubia in

the sixth century C.E.

18. 580 C.E. The calculation is done according to the Seleucid Era, which began in 311 B.C.E. and was widely used in the Near East.

Notes to Document 24 (p. 118–120)

Source: Reprinted from Richard Holton Pierce, "A Sale of an Alodian Slave Girl: a Reexamination of Papyrus Strassburg Inv. 1404," *Symbolae Osloenses* 70 (1995): 159–164, by permission of Scandinavian University Press.

19. Modern el-Ashmunein in Middle Egypt.
20. September 19.
21. The reference is to the annual assessment of land tax. The assessments were numbered serially in fifteen-year cycles during the reign of late Roman emperors and were used to date legal documents. Unfortunately, which emperor's reign is intended cannot be determined so that the papyrus can only be dated generally to the sixth century C.E. on paleographical grounds.
22. Most probably slave-traders, who specialized in Nubian slaves. The existence of such specialist traders suggests a trade of significant size in Nubian slaves.
23. Atalous is called a "Maura" or "Moor," a synonym for Aithiopian with the connotation of dark or black; cf. Frank Snowden, *Blacks in Antiquity: Ethiopians in the Greco-Roman Experience* (Cambridge, MA: Harvard University Press, 1970), 11–12.
24. I.e. from Alwah. As war seems to have been the primary source of slaves in general throughout antiquity, it is likely that Atalous was seized in wars attendent on the hostilities between the various Nubian kingdoms referred to in Documents 21 and 23; cf. S. M. Burstein, "The Nubian Slave Trade in Antiquity: A Suggestion," *Graeco-Africana*, pp. 195–205.
25. The solidus weiged 1/72 of a pound and was the foundation of the late Roman coinage system.

Notes to Document 25 (p. 121–124)

Source: J. H. Feese, *The Library of Photius*, Vol. 1 (New York, 1920), 17–20.

26. This summary of the narrative of Nonnosus is one of the 280 abstracts of works claimed to have been read by Photius, Patriarch of Constantinople

from 858–867 C.E. and 878–886 C.E., contained in the *Bibliotheca* (*Library*).

27. Nonnosus' use of the term "Ethiopia" reflects the transference of the designation from the Nile Valley south of Egypt to modern Ethiopia by Christian writers following the conversion of Ezana in the fourth century C.E.

28. Nonnosus' embassy is to be dated to ca. 530 C.E. Nonnosus' embassy was to three peoples: Roman Arab allies in central Arabia, Axum, and the kingdom of Himyar in the southwestern portion of the Arabian peninsula. Nonnosus' mission was to aid in the recruitment of allies in the Red Sea area for Rome in a war with Persia that had broken out in 527 C.E. (cf. Irfan Shahid, "Byzantium and Kinda," *Byzantinische Zeitschrift* 53 [1960]: 57–73).

29. The origin of the term Saracen is unknown. In late ancient texts such as Nonnosus it refers to the nomadic Arab populations of the Arabian peninsula beyond the Roman frontier (cf. Irfan Shahid, *Rome and the Arabs* [Washington, D.C., 1984], 121–141). Qays was chief of the Chindena (=Kinda) in west central Arabia.

30. The date of this embassy was 502 C.E.

31. Mundhir, chief of the Lakhmids, an Arab tribe in the northwestern portion of the Arabian peninsula.

32. The date of this embassy was 524 C.E.

33. I.e. Constantinople. Nonnosus, like many Byzantine writers, followed the convention of referring to the contemporary realities under the names found in classical Greek literature.

34. The king in question is Kaleb. Nonnosus referred to the king not by his personal name but by his "Ella" name, which he received at his coronation and used as his reign title. In the case of Kaleb that name was Ella Atsbeha which means "he who brought forth the dawn" (cf. Munro-Hay, 159).

35. The exact location of Aue is unknown, but the text suggests that it was somewhere on the Ethiopian plateau (cf. Munro-Hay, 31).

36. June, July, and August; and December, January, and February respectively. Nonnosus used the movement of the sun through the zodiac instead of the months of the solar calendar to indicate the seasons of the year.

37. The Farasan Islands (16′42″ N, 42′ E), the largest islands on the eastern side of the Red Sea. The reference is presumably drawn from Nonnosus' account of his visit to Himyar.

Notes to Document 26 (p. 125–126)

Source: Theophanes, *Chronographia*, Annus mundi 6064. Unpublished translation used by permission of the translator, Dr. Harry Turtledove.

38. 527 C.E.
39. The title Magistrianus identifies Julian as a Roman official subject to the authority of the Master of Offices (*Magister Officiorum*), who was officially in charge of court ceremonial but whose actual responsibilities were much broader and included foreign affairs.
40. The principal source for Julian's embassy is Procopius, *Wars* 1.20. For possible connections between the embassies of Nonnosus and Julian, see Irfan Shahid, "Byzantium and Kinda," *Byzantinische Zeitschrift* 53 [1960]: 62–65.
41. I.e. the Red Sea; cf. Document 19, note 35 for the use of the term "India" in late antiquity to refer the Red Sea and its hinterlands.
42. I.e. Axumites.
43. I.e. Kaleb. Theophanes appears to have confused him with the contemporary Saracen chieftain Arethas (cf. Nonnosus, Document 25).
44. I.e. trade between South Arabia and Egypt would be re-routed via the Axumite road described in Document 15.

Notes to Document 27 (p. 127–132)

Source: Reprinted from "An Eighth-Century Arabic Letter to the King of Nubia" by J. Martin Plumley, *Journal of Egyptian Archaeology* 61 (1975): 242–244, by permission of the Egypt Exploration Society.

45. The *baqt* also provided for free passage for Nubian visitors to Egypt.
46. Until the discovery of this document, the *baqt* was known only from later Arabic historical and legal documents, which were primarily concerned with explaining and justifying the unusual decision to recognize the continuing existence of an unconquered Christian state. The discovery of this document tends to confirm the main details of the later Islamic accounts and to render unlikely the recent theory that the *baqt* was merely an unwritten agreement imposed by the King of Makouria and Nobatia on the defeated Muslims; cf. Jay Spaulding, "Medieval Christian Nubia and the Islamic World: A Reconsideration of the Baqt Treaty," *International Journal of African Historical Studies* 28 (1995): 577–594.
47. The "deputy" was probably the Eparch of Nobatia, the governor of

Lower Nubia, whose residence was at Qasr Ibrim; cf. J. Martin Plumley, "An Eighth Century Arabic Letter to the King of Nubia," *Journal of Egyptian Archaeology* 61 (1975): 245.

48. I.e. the Blemmyes. The Nubians claimed that the Arab merchant was really involved in the sort of raids by Bega/Blemmyes attested in Documents 16–17.

49. The complaint is two-fold: (1) Nubians were behind in the provision of slaves specified in the *baqt* and (2) those they did provide were of inferior quality. The actual number of slaves the Nubians were supposed to provide varies in the Arab sources between 300 and 365. Claims that the Nubians fell behind in meeting this obligation occur frequently and probably reflect the fact that Arabic demands exceeded the capacity of the Nubians to obtain slaves from the region; cf. Spaulding, 591–593.

50. 759 C.E.

SELECT BIBLIOGRAPHY

Adams, William Y., *Nubia: Corridor to Africa* (Princeton, 1977).

Africa in Antiquity: The Arts of Ancient Nubia and the Sudan (Brooklyn, 1978).

Agatharchides of Cnidus, *On the Erythraean Sea*, translated by Stanley M. Burstein (London, 1989).

Burstein, Stanley M., *Graeco-Africana: Studies in the History of Greek Relations with Egypt and Nubia* (New Rochelle, 1995).

Buxton, David, *The Abyssinians* (Southampton, 1970).

Cary, M., and E. H. Warmington, *The Ancient Explorers*, rev. ed. (Harmondsworth, 1963).

Connah, Grahem, *African Civilizations: Precolonial cities and states in tropical Africa: an archaeological perspective* (Cambridge, 1987).

Cosmas Indicopleustes, *The Christian Topography of Cosmas, An Egyptian Monk*, translated by J. W. McCrindle (London, 1898).

Desanges, Jehan, *Recherches sur l'Activité des Méditerranéens aux Confins de l'Afrique* (Paris, 1978).

Eide, Tormod, Tomas Hägg, Richard Holton Pierce and László Török, *Fontes Historiae Nubiorum: Textual Sources for the History of the Middle Nile Region between the Eighth Century BC and the Sixth Century AD*, 2 vols. (Bergen, 1996).

Expedition Magazine 35, 2 [Kush issue] (1993).

Groom, Nigel, *Frankincense and Myrrh: A Study of the Arabian Incense Trade* (London, 1981).

Hable-Sellassie, Sergew, *Ancient and Medieval Ethiopian History to 1270* (Addis Ababa, 1972).

Haynes, Joyce L., *Nubia: Ancient Kingdoms of Africa* (Boston,

1992).

Hintze, Fritz, and Ursula Hintze, *Civilizations of the Ancient Sudan* (Chicago, 1969).

Kendell, Timothy, *Kush: Lost Kingdom of the Nile* (Brockton, 1982).

———, "Sudan's Kingdom of Kush," *National Geographic* 178, 5 (1990): 96–125.

KMT: A Modern Journal of Ancient Egypt 3.3 [Special Nubia issue] (Fall, 1992).

Kobishchanov, Yuri M., *Axum*, translated by Lorraine T. Kapitanoff (University Park, 1979).

Miller, J. Innes, *The Spice Trade of the Roman Empire 29* B.C. *to* A.D. *642* (Oxford, 1969).

Mokhtar, G., *UNESCO General History of Africa: II: Ancient Civilizations of Africa* (Berkeley and Los Angeles, 1981).

Munro-Hay, Stuart, *Aksum: An African Civilization of Late Antiquity* (Edinburgh, 1991).

O'Connor, David, *Ancient Nubia: Egypt's Rival in Africa* (Philadelphia, 1993).

The Periplus Maris Erythraei, edited and translated by Lionel Casson (Princeton, 1989).

Sadr, Karim, *The Development of Nomadism in Ancient Northeast Africa* (Philadelphia, 1991).

Shinnie, P. L., *Meroe: A Civilization of the Sudan* (London: Thames and Hudson, 1967).

Sidebotham, Steven E., *Roman Economic Policy in the Erythra Thalassa: 30* B.C.–A.D. *217* (Leiden, 1986).

Snowden, Frank M., Jr., *Blacks in Antiquity: Ethiopians in the Greco-Roman Experience* (Cambridge, Mass., 1970).

———, *Before Color Prejudice: The Ancient View of Blacks* (Cambridge, Mass., 1983).

Speidel, M., "Nubia's Roman Garrison," *Aufstieg und*

Niedergang der Römischen Welt, II.10.1 (Berlin, 1988), 767–798.

Taylor, John H., *Egypt and Nubia* (Cambridge, Mass., 1991).

Thompson, L., and Ferguson, J., eds., Africa in Classical Antiquity (Ibadan, 1969).

Török, László, *Economic Offices and Officials in Meroitic Nuba (A Study in Territorial Administration of the Late Meroitic Kingdom)* (Budapest, 1979).

———, *Late Antique Nubia: History and archaeology of the southern neighbour of Egypt in the 4th–6th c.* A.D. (Budapest, 1987).

———, *Meroe: Six Studies on the Cultural Identity of an Ancient African State* (Budapest, 1995).

Trigger, Bruce, *Nubia under the Pharaohs* (London, 1976).

Updegraff, R. T. "The Blemmyes I: The Rise of the Blemmyes and the Roman Withdrawal from Nubia under Diocletian (with Additional Remarks by L. Török, Budapest)," *Aufstieg und Niedergang der Römischen Welt*, II.10.1 (Berlin, 1988), 44–106.

Vantini, John, *The Excavations at Faras: A Contribution to the History of Christian Nubia* (Bologna, 1970).

Vercoutter, Jean, *et. al. The Image of the Black in Western Art: I: From the Pharaohs to the Fall of the Roman Empire* (New York: Morrow, 1976).

Welsby, Derek A., *The Kingdom of Kush: The Napatan and Meroitic Empires* (London, 1996).

Wildung, Dietrich, *Sudan: Ancient Kingdoms of the Nile*, translated by Peter Der Manuelian (New York, 1997).

Zabcar, L. V., *Apedemak: Lion God of Meroe* (Warminster, 1975).

INDEX